W9-AOA-605

Also by Dan Bongino

Spygate: The Attempted Sabotage
of Donald J. Trump

Exonerated: The Failed Takedown
of President Donald Trump by the Swamp

Follow the Money: The Shocking Deep State
Connections of the Anti-Trump Cabal

THE **GIFT** OF **FAILURE**

THE **GIFT** OF **FAILURE**

*(And I'll rethink the title
if this book fails!)*

DAN BONGINO

Liberatio
Protocol

A LIBERATIO PROTOCOL BOOK
An Imprint of Post Hill Press

The Gift of Failure:
(And I'll rethink the title if this book fails!)
© 2023 by Dan Bongino
All Rights Reserved

ISBN: 979-8-88845-062-8
ISBN (eBook): 979-8-88845-063-5

Cover design by Conroy Accord
Cover photo courtesy of Patty D. Marchesi

Post Hill Press
New York • Nashville
posthillpress.com

Published in the United States of America
1 2 3 4 5 6 7 8 9 10

I dedicate this book to my wife and children;
they've never failed me

Contents

Preface

I did not set out to write a self-help book per se. This is more what I call a "motivational memoir" about how to use failure to your advantage. Listen, failure is a natural part of the learning process: I talk about it all the time. Failure is not the opposite of success; it is a necessary part of the journey towards success. Every failure can provide us with an opportunity to learn and grow and can help us improve our skills and approach.

Part of the reason I wrote this book was to show that when we fail, we can use that experience to gain valuable feedback about what went wrong and what we can do differently next time. This feedback can help us improve and avoid similar mistakes in the future. I make my mistakes, you create your own mistakes, but we can deal with them in similar ways.

Something I learned early in life is that facing and overcoming failure can also help us build resilience—the ability to bounce back from adversity. The latest buzz term for that is "grit." By learning from our failures and persevering through difficult times, we can develop the strength and confidence to face future challenges with a new and more refined skill set.

I've had big successes but even more big failures. And that's okay. Failure can help us redefine success by allowing us to reassess our goals and values. By acknowledging and accepting our failures, we can gain a clearer understanding of what we truly want and need to achieve fulfillment in our lives.

Why do I actually love failure? Because failure can inspire us to work harder and smarter towards our goals. Through these failures, I had a tough enough time helping myself. But again, I'd rather repeat them here so that you can perhaps benefit from the failures you may encounter. I'll tell you, I gained something by writing this book. I hope your experience is similar after reading it.

Introduction

If you listen to my radio show or podcast, you may have heard me say that I wasn't going to write any more books. So you might be wondering, what's going on right now?

It's a fair question, so I'll start at the beginning. At least I think this is the beginning. Maybe it's just the end of the beginning. Hopefully, it's not the beginning of the end. I guess it will all be dependent on what my next failure is and how I respond to it.

September 22, 2022. I was back in New York City, where I was born and spent most of my childhood. We were walking in Times Square. Ever since it took on that name back in 1904 when the *New York Times* moved into the building where the New Year's Eve ball would eventually drop from, Times Square for millions of people has been like a crossroads of the world.

I've had my own experiences there, and I do have a lot of feelings about that bustling epicenter in the heart of Manhattan. A lot of it goes back to when I was a young police cadet. I had taken some bad advice from an officer who was kind of a mentor to me. He said, "Hey man, if you're going to be a cop you need to be a cop in Midtown." So he sent me to the Midtown South Precinct. You want to talk about an epic failure: I was totally lost. I was an intern cadet; nobody knew who I was or what I was supposed to be doing. The desk sergeant had that "who the hell are you?" look on his face. As for me, I didn't even know how to get there from where I lived in Queens. Lesson number one: when you get a job, it's helpful if you can actually figure out how to find the place.

I just didn't think this thing through at all. I was unfamiliar with the subways. I also lived in a two-fare zone which meant there wasn't a subway stop in my neighborhood, so I had to take a bus to the train. It was a pain. I knew so little about the transit system that I couldn't even find my way there. Failure!

So, Times Square always held this special place in my heart because it was the site of such an early failure. I missed the chance to properly evaluate the situation, and maybe ask some questions (like how do you get there?), and it's also helpful if they actually know you work there when you do finally show up. So I worked there one day and that was it. I called the officer who recommended it and said, "I gotta get out of here." And I did. Lucky for me, something opened up in the patrol borough of Queens North. It may have only been a data entry position, but it was in a cool unit called the Pattern Identification Module. It was one of the New York Police Department's earliest efforts to profile criminals. It turned out great for me. I would sit there all day analyzing patterns of criminals, and it helped prepare me for what I would be doing later on as a Secret Service agent. So my failure with directions and ability to navigate the transit system actually produced something good for me.

Anyway, I'm there with my wife and daughter right where the ball drops, watching myself on the big Times Square jumbotron. We had just finished ringing the Nasdaq bell to launch Rumble.

And it got me thinking…

The vicissitudes in life...the ups and downs...the circles inside the circles got me thinking about the Secret Service protection models, bubbles inside of bubbles inside of bubbles... like how the hell am I back here in Times Square ushering in a multi-billion-dollar company after not hacking it in this very spot as a cadet?

Yet here I was. Back in Times Square. A place that was also emblematic of what the Republican Party could do if you put them in power. When Rudolph Giuliani came in, he helped save the place. He took a public safety failure and flipped it over, creating a tourist Mecca.

So taking this company public, and looking up at that big screen at my made-for-radio face, I felt like I had made it. My wife, daughter, and I were walking back to the hotel afterward, in the pouring rain, and I was still in a little bit of shock over what we had just accomplished. Me being me, I start reading my social media accounts. Some people out there claim they don't care what people say, but I'm not one of them. I read everything. I don't have any of that faux bravado. I don't pretend or fake it. I care. I have callouses, and I do have thick skin, but I still care. In the face of this massive success, I was getting a bunch of comments saying what a failure I was. "He ran for office three times and lost! *Failure.*" I looked at my wife and said, "If this is what failure looks like, more please."

And we laughed.

Walking back, dodging puddles, squeezing through box-blocking gridlock, we had some more time to chat. I said to her, "You know what would be a great book? About how failure can be a gift. How failure can be a springboard, depending on how you look at it. If you look at it as an impenetrable obstacle, then that's what it's going to become. But if you look at it as an opportunity to learn something, and you start looking for other opportunities as a result, good things can happen."

It's like a parallax: Two people see the same thing differently. One can look at failure as a dead end. Another can see a new door.

I said, "Maybe I should write that book." And she said, "Really? I thought you weren't gonna write another book. Clearly, you are about to fail on that promise."

Touché.

I felt inspired as we kept walking. I began cataloging all of the successes that had worked out for me both in my professional and my personal life. I came to a realization that practically every single one of them was born out of a massive failure.

Not getting into medical school…what happened with the big-tech takedown of Parler…missing out on the First Lady's detail in the Secret Service…and many more stories…

Look, here's the hard truth: I have no extra special skills. I'm not fast. I have an average IQ. I think I have a good social IQ but not an overly impressive intellectual IQ. The bottom line is there's simply nothing remarkable about me or my backstory. So maybe this book could be special because if a guy like me who is not the best looking, fastest, or strongest, or isn't the smartest but has a lot of grit and never views failure as an obstacle but a good opportunity—if I can get here, then assuredly people who are smarter and better looking can do even more.

With each block, I kept thinking of more failures in my life that I had somehow parlayed into something good. I have always viewed rain as a sign of luck, a cleansing force, and on this day, it was helping me reveal more in my mind by washing away the dust of time.

That walk to the hotel became more than just a rain-sodden slog. It became one part time machine and another part inspirational reservoir. Times Square never lets me down. I always learn something there.

Okay, so I guess this is the beginning of the beginning. I may have failed in my assertion that I wouldn't be writing any more books in the near future. But I think something good came out of that failure: an opportunity to tell you some stories that I hope will inspire you.

Go figure.

1

"It is hard to fail, but it is worse never to have tried to succeed."

—THEODORE ROOSEVELT

I learned the lesson early. I think everybody learns it early, but we tend to either forget about it or block it out because most people don't like dealing with failure. For me, it was like a lightning bolt. I could not help but be affected by it. Failure kicked my ass early when I needed it to, and I'm still affected by this moment today.

It's not how you look at things. It's what you *do* with the failure—how do you act, what are the action items, what are you *doing* with the failure? The "*do*" matters.

I was a huge baseball fan. But, because of Major League Baseball's failure to keep excessively destructive politics out of their game, this sport has since alienated me.

One of my earliest lessons was a good one, and it taught me that failure can be a gift. It's all about how you look at things. It happened on the baseball diamond. Let's face it, baseball is all about failure: Striking out. Committing errors. It's all baked into

1

the game. How many times have you watched a guy commit an error at the most critical moment of the game? He's worked his whole life to be in that position. He boots a routine grounder when they need that out more than anything. I always look at that guy and think, What is he going to do next? Is he going to let it crush him? Or is he going to quickly analyze what went wrong and what good can come out of that moment? Today, it's just how I roll. But I had to learn that. And like I said, it started on the baseball diamond.

Like every other kid my age growing up in Queens, I had dreams of being a ball player. I mean come on. Whether you were a Mets fan or a Yankees fan, we were surrounded by baseball. I was a Yankees fan. Don Mattingly was my guy. Mattingly was a doer. Unchallengeable work ethic, and very little talk. Those Yankees teams that were around when I was growing up didn't do very well throughout the 1980s. I mean, they had great players, including my guy Mattingly, Dave Winfield, Rickey Henderson, and plenty of other stars. But they failed throughout the decade. After losing to the Dodgers in the 1981 World Series, the Yankees started their longest absence from the playoffs since 1921. The 1980s was the first decade since the 1910s that the Yankees did not win at least *two* World Series. You could write an entire book about how they overcame that failure to come back and dominate in the 1990s. But that's a different story for a different person to write. (Even the Mets managed to win a series in the '80s. Though I still wonder if the great Bill Buckner was ever able to overcome his now-mythical failure of game six in the '86 series when he misplayed Mookie Wilson's grounder.)

My family was all about sports. My brothers and stepbrother were all good athletes, and we ate, drank, and slept sports. All of us. Sometimes my dad would take us to Yankee Stadium. The shrine. There was nothing like that old yard.

So, I was eleven years old, and I had a cousin who was about eight years older than me. Steve, who would go on to become a fireman and with whom I'm still close, was like an idol to me at that age because of what an amazing athlete he was. Hockey, football, baseball, whatever—he was simply freakish. A beast. Steve was an easy hero to have.

One time Steve brought me down to one of my first Little League games. My mom was busy and Steve was happy to help. My coach, Jim, was a good guy. Candidly, I was already a pretty terrible player who had learned to deal with many failures on the field, but Jim always made sure I got in the game (albeit hidden out in right field where I couldn't do too much damage). Very few balls got hit to right field back then. So we were getting clobbered pretty good in this particular game, and I had an idea: I wanted to pitch. My stepbrother was a very good pitcher. I'd watched him enough, and I had tossed a solid Wiffle ball game or two in my time. What could go wrong? Plus, with Steve out there, I knew this would impress him if I did well. And that meant a lot to me.

"Coach, can I get in there and pitch?" Jim's eyebrows went up. "You can pitch?" I nodded with all the confidence I could muster. "Okay," he said. "Take the mound next inning."

The first thing I realized on the mound: it is *lonely* out there. Just you, the ball, and all eyes fixed on you. It's all about you. People in the stands are watching you. Your team is watching you. The opposition is watching you. Nothing happens until you release the ball. You're alone in the same way a boxer is alone in the ring. But at least he has an opponent. Anyway, what the hell? This was my shot. I was gonna show Steve.

So much for the plan.

It was a horror show. I think they batted around before I even got an out. If I did even get an out. I was yanked, and I remember thinking I had blown it. I looked up and saw Steve's face in the stands, and it crushed me. I can still picture his expression today, and it haunts me a little bit. I had let my hero down. I had let my team down. I had let myself down. I had no business being out there. I gambled by asking to pitch that day, and I lost. I went big, and I failed big.

Bongino, thy name is Failure.

After the game, Steve drove me home, and I was pretty quiet. I was just so embarrassed. Call it an inner rebellion. Call it an epiphany. Call it whatever you want. But I decided that I was not going to be a scrub. I was not going to fold. Maybe I was not meant to be a pitcher, but that was okay. That failure was resonating very heavily in my head and in my heart. And I distinctly remember thinking, I have to do something with this. This feeling is power-ful. It has the strength to break me, but I'm not going to let it. I'm going to use it to my advantage.

I'm going to let that failure motivate me.

When I woke up the next day, I could see it in front of me: I'm going to be an outfielder and a great hitter. That was it. As I said, my stepbrother was a phenomenal pitcher. In fact, he was drafted by the Mets organization and played for a few years. So there would be no competing with him. He was a pitcher, and I was not. That was okay. But I knew I had to focus. I had to take that failure and pound it into something. Literally. So I got a batting tee, and I set it up in my backyard. Literally. (And you know I hate that word, so consider this a failure I will have to work on.) Now, when I say backyard, I'm not talking about a field of dreams. In my young mind, it may have been Yankee Stadium, but in reality, we lived in one of the small Queens row houses—"Archie Bunker houses" as I call them because they look like the opening credits from the TV show, *All in the Family.*

These were houses right smack next to each other that had a little strip of open space in between them. And that was it. So I couldn't hit the ball off the tee into the neighbor's yard. I would be chasing balls all day and breaking a few windows in between. My family, like many other families in the neighborhood, used to dry the clothes by hanging them on a clothesline. Very few neighbors had dryers. So I went and found a thick ten-by-ten blanket inside the house, draped it over the clothesline, and then would hit the baseballs off the tee, smacking them right into the blanket. I couldn't afford new baseballs, so I used old ones that had been thrown away by the team. The covers were coming off them for crying out loud, but I didn't care. They were good enough. I would hit balls off that tee from day into night until my hands got bloody. Hundreds and hundreds of baseballs thudding into that old blanket. Smack. Thud. Smack. Thud. Over and over.

Then I would pick them all up and start again with our dog, a loveable shepherd mutt named Chipper, keeping me company. (He was named by my brother who loved Atlanta Braves legend Chipper Jones.) Soon after, I found a big piece of heavy industrial pipe, maybe three feet long, and I would swing that thing all day long before hitting off the tee. And guess what happened? After a year or so of this conditioning, things started to pay off. I became a so-so Little League player. Then a good player. And then I was the best player on my Sgt. Miller Post-Ridgewood-Glendale-Middle Village Little League team. And then I was the terror of Juniper

Valley Park in Middle Village, where we played. I could crush the ball, and I was a strong fielder, as well.

That was my first lesson in how to harness the power of failure. My first realization was that there actually could be something positive from the pain of failure. But baseball wasn't done teaching me lessons. At sixteen, I was picked by an influential man in my life, Coach Stan, to play American Legion Baseball on a team called the Warriors. He was a tough guy. Stoic, Coach Stan wasted few words, except when he would put you on blast for screwing up. As good as I was in Little League, I had to work myself up on this team, and it was like going back to square one. But that was okay. I liked the challenge, and I succeeded. Eventually, I worked my way to batting third in the lineup, which is the best place to be. If you know anything about baseball, you know that batting third is badass. Everyone knows you're the most dangerous hitter. You step into the box, and the outfielders all back up a little bit. But I would soon get knocked off my horse, learning another lesson about failure. Or at least the perception of failure.

We were playing a game at Abraham Lincoln High School in Brooklyn. I'm playing left field and a guy hits a fly ball to me. Bases are loaded, we're up about ten runs, and there's nobody out. I see the ball drifting foul so let it drop. I didn't want the guy on third to tag up. I thought this was the smart move. Textbook, right? Don't let that guy on third score. Guess again. I could hear Coach Stan screaming at me, "Come on, guy!" from the dugout. What had I done wrong? Well, after we *finally* got out of the inning, I learned. He grabbed me by the shoulders when I got into the dugout and started yelling at me, "We are up by ten freaking runs. You catch that damn ball and give the pitcher an out!"

The lesson? Everything in life is on the margin. No rule can be written in stone. Under most conditions, you let that foul ball drop. But not in that situation. I did what I *thought* was the right thing. But I was wrong. So I had failed. And that was an eye-opener for me. Coach was right. The out was more important at that point than the run. You can't take anything for granted. You have to be in the moment and think specifically about what is going on. Nothing is black-and-white.

There's just something about baseball. I learned lots of lessons as a young man thanks to the national pastime. Every pitch contains some kind of opportunity to learn. But nothing started preparing me for life like that first time out on the mound when I got shelled. That was a revelation. That was the first time in my life when I realized that if you had the right attitude, then failure wasn't just the necessary rite of passage; it was an essential growth tool that would help me achieve things beyond my wildest imagination.

As I sit here thinking about this now, I'm reminded of the adage of baseball: "The best hitters in the world fail seventy percent of the time." I don't think that's true. Just because you don't get a hit to get on base doesn't mean you failed as a batter. If you hit the ball and it becomes a ground out or a fly out, I don't think that's a failure. You did what you were supposed to do. You put the ball in play. If you hit a screamer down third base and the guy makes a phenomenal play on it, you didn't fail. You hit the ball. That's a success in itself. Once you hit the ball, it's out of your hands. You did what you were supposed to do.

Today, although baseball and I are separated due to woke politics (en route to a divorce), it still holds a special place in my heart. It also remains a powerful metaphor in defining not just how to make the most out of failure, but also what the word even means. And it certainly helped prepare me for the next big challenges in my life.

2

"My great concern is not whether you have failed,
but whether you are content with your failure."

—ABRAHAM LINCOLN

think that early failures in life tend to be the most traumatic because we don't have any life skills or coping skills to deal with failure at a young age. We have no frames of reference to compare anything to. Everything seems more amplified because we haven't yet developed a deep context for the experiences we are going through.

Something happened to me when I was in grade school that I remember as if it happened yesterday. Oftentimes, I can't remember what I had for lunch yesterday. But this childhood event is still so vivid to me and yes, traumatic, because when it happened, I had nothing to compare it to. It was all new.

It started when my mom came into my class, pulled me out of school, and told me matter-of-factly, "We are leaving our neighborhood and moving to Queens." You have to understand; I did not grow up in an urban environment. We lived way out in Suffolk County on Long Island, in Smithtown. Back then, it was about as rural as you could get in the tri-state area. To me, it might as well have been like *Little House on the Prairie*. Not much crime. No hassles. And certainly no violent fighting between kids. We lived on an isolated street called Rose Lane, which created an even more protected environment. I loved it out there. What wasn't to love? You could roam the neighborhood and the open spaces without a care in the world. As long as you were home before dark, everything was okay. And even if it was after dark, no big deal. Nothing bad ever seemed to happen out there in that idyllic wonderland. And now, in the blink of an eye, everything was changing. My parents were getting divorced. That's what predicated the move. So I was plucked out of my bucolic bliss and immediately thrust into the netherworld of Myrtle Avenue in Queens. It's hard to even describe the degree of culture shock that this represented for me.

We moved into a small, cramped apartment over a bar that my family ran. The nighttime sounds of crickets, katydids, and tree frogs that had lulled me to sleep for years were now replaced by sirens, car horns, and random street corner arguments that echoed across the night. We had no air conditioning, which made things even more oppressive and claustrophobic. Myrtle Avenue was a major thoroughfare that never seemed to quiet down. My mother couldn't take it either, and so after a few years, when I was in about seventh grade, we moved nearby to an area called Liberty Park. It wasn't perfect. But it was at least far enough away from the action that you could get a decent night's rest.

Growing up in Smithtown, the only fighting I was exposed to was what I watched on *The Dukes of Hazzard*, G.I. Joe cartoons, or maybe a Chuck Norris movie. That was it. Fighting wasn't real.

It was cartoonish, and everybody always walked away intact. It did not seem like a big deal. As I would soon learn, nothing prepares you for fighting like living in the city. There's almost no way around it. And getting clipped in the face the first time is a life-defining moment. I'm often reminded of the old Mike Tyson line when someone asked him about the plan that one of his opponents had going into a fight against him. Tyson responded with something like, "Everyone has a plan until they get punched in the face." Words to live by. Iron Mike, a Brooklyn kid, could not have been more right.

Coming in from the "country," (and to you folks who actually grew up in the country, who are probably laughing at this right now, believe me, to this tri-state kid, it felt like the country), I had never been in a fight. Hell, I don't think I had ever been in an argument. Things were just that quiet, way out on "the island" as city kids called it. But in my new urban jungle reality, I was soon exposed to an entirely different existence. I don't think we had been in that new place in Liberty Park for more than a month when I was confronted by Steve. He was "that kid." The tough guy on the block. Every neighborhood has one. But in my unsuspecting mind, he was not a problem. I was a big kid, and I had watched enough ninja movies where I had figured that I was the tough guy on the block, and I would marshal those special ninja powers in the event I needed them. I saw them on TV and so they had to be real, right?

This is where not having any prior experience creates a completely artificial, even somewhat delusional, view of the world. Such is youth. Steve moved in on me one day because that's simply what the alpha male in a neighborhood like that does. All I can say is that it was over quickly. Two hits. He hit me and I hit the ground. And it hurt. Not only did it hurt, but it also threw my body out of whack. On television, people who got into fights did not go through what I was going through. Losing your breath, sucking wind, pain radiating through your whole body, the humiliation, the embarrassment, the shock to your entire nervous system— on TV they leave that part out. And then once the physical pain begins to ebb, the deep and dark sense of humiliation completely envelops you. In front of all of the new friends I had been making in the neighborhood, I was now "that guy who got beat up by Steve." In my mind, I may have started like some kind of Chuck Norris–styled ninja, but now I was just the guy who got beat up by Steve. Once the dust had settled, over the course of the next few months, getting my ass kicked by Steve became a seminal event in my life. It was eating away at my soul. To this day, it's one of the top five most deeply impactful moments in my life. (If you listen to my radio show, you know I love lists.)

And that has to do with what I did in reaction to the beating.

I was a proud kid back then. I was confident. I believed in myself. And so the fact that I got taken out so easily pissed me off. I had failed to prepare for this inevitable moment in my life where violence would come my way, and I vowed to myself from that moment on that I would never negotiate from a point of weakness in a violent confrontation. That was not going to happen. Nor was I going to let somebody get the better of me without being fully and completely prepared to fight back. There's nothing wrong with losing a fight if you're prepared and if there's no other way out of it. But there is absolutely something wrong with losing a fight that you should not have been in and that you got in because of faux bravado. And there's nothing worse than walking away and knowing you did so from a point of weakness.

This became the impetus for me to fall in love with martial arts.

From a practical perspective, if you don't how to fight and defend yourself, then that's on you. You let yourself down, and you let the people around you down. Don't believe in nonsense. Your adrenaline isn't going to rescue you from a violent interaction against a trained fighter. Nothing is going to save you. This isn't the movies. No special powers are going to come to you if you say the right words. What's going to happen is that you are going to get your ass kicked, and it's not going to stop until the guy fighting you decides that he's done kicking your ass.

I'm not saying you have to become a UFC (Ultimate Fighting Championship) heavyweight champion. Not even close. Only that you need to be able to defend yourself and your loved ones in an increasingly dangerous world.

That street corner failure of getting my ass kicked by Steve drove me so crazy that I threw myself completely and without any hesitation into a variety of martial arts disciplines. I experimented with everything from tae kwon do to karate and though I felt myself becoming stronger and smarter, it wasn't until I found boxing that I felt like I had discovered my saving grace. What I found with martial arts was that you practiced all of these cool moves, but the hard reality was that it felt hard for me to apply all of that to real-world situations. Everything was very choreographed and orchestrated. But with boxing, you knew right away what the score was. When you got in the ring to spar with somebody, you knew quickly whether you sucked or not. You also learned what you had to do to get better. A couple of shots to the liver will teach you that fast. If you've ever gotten hit in the liver, you know what I mean. Fighting in the street is not that different than sparring. I wanted to know how to fight, and how to win.

I was becoming a strong boxer with good offense but atrocious defense—my defense was getting punched in the face. I ate a lot of punches with my skull, which is maybe why my head is shaped like a box. But then when the UFC stuff started getting popular, I decided to change paths. I saw what was happening to conventional boxers when they got in the ring with trained ground fighters. I was comfortable with my hands now and what I could do as a boxer, but once I started noticing what happened when a guy took you down to the ground, I knew I needed a new path. Brazilian jujitsu became the ticket for me. It took a long time. In Brazilian jujitsu, you may lose ten thousand times before you start to finally figure out how to win. It's like riding a bike. You don't know how to do it until you know how to do it, and you can never explain how you did it. One day, you just get it. And then you learn valuable lessons: "Get on top." That's rule number one. Get on top and stay on top. And if you can't get on top then rule number two is "see rule number one."

For the next twenty years or so of my life, I was dedicated to Brazilian jujitsu, on and off due to health issues. I just loved it. The irony of this whole situation (born out of a failure after being humiliated by Steve) is that today, all of the years I've spent boxing, with Brazilian jujitsu, and so on, have caused enough damage to my body that I'm not even sure I can respond effectively anymore to a physical crisis.

Maybe I just overdid it over the years. That's a big part of my personality. Overdoing it. If you can do it, you can overdo it. And then you can overdo it some more. And then some more after that. That's just how I roll. People always say, "Know your limitations." My answer to that has always been, "If you know your limitations, they will limit you." So that becomes stupid advice. The point is to push through your limitations and achieve something higher and bolder. At least that's how I think about it.

But I'm not going to bullshit you because that's not me. Paula asked me recently what I would tell my twenty-year-old self if I could go back in time. (More advice I would have given my younger self: stay tuned until the end of the book. You'll see what I mean.) Would I recommend taking on more of a sense of moderation, especially when it came to training? When I first started lifting weights, guys in the gym would tell me, "You don't need to do ten sets at that weight." And I would say, "No, it's all about effort. I don't want to do the minimum." I didn't want to appear weak. Looking back, the irony is that it would not have been weak. It would have been "being efficient." Why do unnecessary work that could cause unnecessary damage? Training is all about efficiency. I know that now. I did not know it back then.

In between finishing this book and the time you're taking right now to read it, I will have had several surgeries related to my physical training over the years. That's on me. It's how I'm wired. No matter what I would tell my twenty-year-old self, I'm not sure I would change anything. Even if I knew it was going to hurt me.

As I have shared on my radio show, I struggle occasionally with depression. It runs in my family. It's hard to describe what happens when that black cloud begins looming overhead for no quantifiable reason. I have a great life, I have a great family, and I love what I do. But out of nowhere, it just sometimes happens. There's no rhyme or reason to it. I spoke to a friend about it who deals with this kind of stuff, and she said to me, "Dan, you have a lot of anger." She was right. I did and I still do. We were talking about a *60 Minutes* report that I had seen about how taking magic mushrooms could be an effective measure for curbing depression. But she said to me, "You don't know what those feelings are tied to and if you cut them out, figure out a way to remove them, yes you may not be depressed. But you may become a different person." In my mind, I think I'd rather live with the pain and be my authentic self. The arthritis that I have today may create discomfort, but it also represents the right of passage. Battle scars. It reminds me of the pain I had to deal with a long time ago. If I removed the anger and aggression, how would that filter down into the rest of my life? Would I no longer be as entrepreneurial? Would I no longer be as passionate about things that are important to me?

I will admit that the concept of moderation is something that I am beginning to embrace at this point in my life. But I think this is the appropriate time to embrace moderation. Way back, I don't think it would have been the right move. I don't think it would have helped propel me through the depths of despair and humiliation that I needed to conquer on my own. We never stop growing. We never stop learning. At least that's the theory I ascribe to. I learned as a kid that getting your ass kicked can go one of two ways. It can relegate you into the shadows for the rest of your life and make you afraid of the world. Or, it can motivate you to conquer not just the demons on the outside, lurking on neighborhood street corners, but also the demons within.

Steve, wherever you are, I begrudgingly offer you a small thanks for what you did to me that day. Without that failure, I'm not sure this book would even exist today.

3

"Failure is success in progress."

—ALBERT EINSTEIN

My short time in the New York City Police Department was marked by repeated failures. I didn't know a lot when I joined the force. I was young and cocky. I was at that age where you have an inverse proportionality between what you know and what you think you know. We get older and look back and realize, for the most part, just how naïve we were. It's a weird dynamic in our lives. If we only knew then what we know now...but in a way that represents the theme of this book, because if we had all of the answers, we wouldn't fail. And if we didn't fail, we wouldn't learn. I can't stress this enough. Winning will never teach you as much as failing. As I have worked on this book, it has become so clear to me just how vital the failure process is, especially when I think back to this time in my life. I thought I knew everything, but I had none of the special insights that come with age.

This was about 1995. I had caught a break early. I was in the NYPD cadet program before becoming an officer, which was a paid internship. As I referenced earlier in the book, one of my original failures was not even being able to find the precinct in Manhattan during my first assignment as a cadet. Thankfully, I was able to get out of that assignment and get transferred to the 114th Precinct in Astoria, Queens. It was perfect: a short commute from where I lived in Middle Village, so it could not have been any more convenient.

That two-year-or-so internship earned me a lot of interesting experience. There was one situation that I wasn't that crazy about, however. Believe it or not, I had a baby face back then. That's right. *This* mug. Baby face. So what they wanted me to do was to go to bars to check out the operations—to see if I would get carded. And if I didn't, then they would go in there and give the place a summons. I think of this as my "Fredo" moment. I'm talking about Fredo, the weak, less intelligent Corleone brother played so beautifully by John Cazale in the movie *The Godfather*.

Understand, my family owned and operated a bar. It's a tough business even on the best of nights. So I felt like a total traitor. A spineless turncoat. I wasn't just betraying my family, I was betraying every saloon, every dive bar, and every neighborhood tavern in New York City. These were my people. And I was in there trying to get them busted? After a couple of these moments where I walked out of the bar and reported to the sergeant if they had not asked me for an ID, I realized I had to do something about it. So, several times, even if I was not asked for ID, I told the cops that I was. Maybe that's a failure on my part. But I couldn't help it. I'm guessing the statute of limitations has probably run out after all those years, so the bar can't get in trouble (nor can I—although I'm not a lawyer, so this may be a new failure to deal with).

The way it works in the NYPD is that the day you get your gun and shield is also the day you find out where you are going to be working. That can go several ways. Ideally, and I know this is some inside baseball, when you are a young cop, you want to be assigned to an area that has both a cool nightlife and a rough part of town so you can do cop stuff. Nobody wants to go to a precinct where there is no crime because that's not why you became a cop. You want to chase bad guys.

We call the best precincts "hook houses." Usually, to get into one of those, you had to have a father or uncle who was a deputy inspector or something to "hook you up." One of my best friends, Brian, got placed in the greatest precinct of all which was in Bayside. That meant he could work a solid night and then go party with the boys. But he had hooks. I didn't have hooks to get me into one of those more desirable precincts. But other guys didn't have the seniority that came with my time in the cadet program. I also had some arrogance and hubris that I also brought along from that internship (and by some, I mean a lot!). I figured that would be good enough to get me into one of the more sought-after precincts.

I could not have been more wrong.

During my time in the cadet program, I did something that inadvertently got me in trouble. I had signed in at a certain time, which locked out a chief from signing in because she had come in late. I was on time. She was late. But from what I heard, she got so pissed off at me that it resulted in a vendetta of sorts. As someone on the inside later pointed out to me, she was going to make me pay for locking her out. Which, again, was in no way a failure on my part.

So, the day we got our guns and shields, I heard them call out the precinct where I would be working. It was the Seventy-Fifth Precinct in East New York, Brooklyn. Back then, this was the absolute worst of the worst. The most dangerous spot perhaps anywhere on the East Coast. Today it's better, but back then there was no way around it. It was simply the most threatening precinct you could be assigned to. It had essentially no redeeming qualities. Social life? Forget about it. It was all crime all the time. Cops in that precinct back then had T-shirts made based on the old 1010 WINS news radio slogan, which used to say, "You give us 22 minutes, we'll give you the world." These T-shirts read, "You give us 22 minutes, we'll give you a homicide."

Sometimes it didn't even take ten minutes.

So, when they were calling our names and they said, "Bongino, seventy-five," it was a true kick in the balls. I knew it was bad by the collective reaction that I heard from the other cops around me: "Oof!" Everybody knew it was grim. Those two numbers were the worst you could get. It took me a little while to digest and process the news. I had been busting my ass to get seniority, and this was where they stuck me? There were only two kinds of people that got stuck in the seventy-five. "Hairbags," which is what we called old senior cops who complained about everything, and rookies that they hated and wanted to punish. I had no recourse. And again, as I learned later, supposedly this was payback for my "non-mistake mistake" that evidently prompted that chief to take a hit out on me in the form of shipping me out to the worst, most foreboding spot on the NYC map. It was a place where we were warned to look out for "airmail" when we walked into a housing project. What was airmail? I'd heard it was when they would dump bags of cement out the windows from the top floors to try and kill you as you were walking into the building. I thought they were exaggerating.

Until it happened to a guy.

If there was any silver lining to it at all, it's that working in the seventy-five got the willies out of the way quickly. What are the willies? Not something from a porn movie. It's that fear and anxiety you have being in a bad situation. And the thing about the seventy-five was that you were *always* in a bad situation, from the moment you stepped into the precinct. So, you could either learn to get the willies out of the way or you could just resign. But there was no "option C." And every cop in the city knew it. The place turned you into an automatic badass. There was no way to head out there and stay clear of fisticuffs, shootings, and the like, so whatever happened, I knew I was going to quickly turn into a real cop. I got a sense of that right away when we were all assigned to head back into Manhattan one night to cover the lighting of the Rockefeller Center Christmas tree. When I and the other guys from the seventy-five got there, surrounded by cops from all over the city, and they took roll call, let's just say when they saw who was from the seventy-five, we got a lot of respect. I liked that. They gave you the "cop look," that knowing nod.

We were the tough guys. Sure, that meant we got a lot of shit assignments because it was presumed that we could handle them, and we were kept out of view for the most part because of how tough and unpresentable everybody assumed we were, but that was okay. It was all part of the seventy-five street cred that I was starting to value.

So, what's the failure? Well, there's a patrol guide that we all followed that puts down on paper the formal rules of how things are supposed to work. Makes sense. You need to have a basic manual of exactly what needs to happen, for a lot of reasons. Not the least of which is that we are living in such a litigious society today, and it was becoming more and more important to protect officers from frivolous accusations. But 99 percent of what we did out on the street involved a lot of personal discretion. We would encounter very sensitive, very in-the-moment events. The kind of stuff you simply can't describe in a patrol guide.

One night, I was out on a call with a guy named Jason. Good guy, I knew him from the academy, but also a very aggressive young guy. Jason was somebody who dreamed of going to the seventy-five. He just wanted to be a "real" cop. I would bet he's the only guy in the history of the NYPD who dreamed of finding himself in that godforsaken precinct. So, he and I were out on a foot post together after midnight, which is a truly dangerous time for any place in that area. We didn't have the support of a car. A car in that situation is a big mobile barrier. It gives you the ability to escape, evade, and get away from dangerous people. But on a foot post, you don't have that. You were just walking around in the middle of the night, and in this case, also in the dead of winter.

Jason and I saw this kid doing drugs. We confronted him after letting Central (911 operator) know our location. (God forbid if something broke bad, they would know where to dispatch other officers to.) A few minutes later, two older, old-school, salty cops (whose sector we were in) pulled up. I'm talking guys who have probably arrested a thousand people in their careers. We were freezing our asses off out there, busting this guy's chops over a low-level drug offense, and one of the older cops called me over. I didn't want to leave Jason alone with the perp, but the older cop was adamant. When I got over there, he said to me, "Listen, you seriously think it's a good idea to bust this kid's balls over what he is doing?" Hey, it said in our manual that this is what we were supposed to do. I was full of myself. I was arrogant. I was doing things by the book as I was taught. The cop continued, "Look, there are a lot of external things that don't apply to the guide. You might need this kid at some point to help you out in this neighborhood. It can save your life if you develop smart relationships. This is one of the deadliest and most dangerous precincts, so you need to play any angle that you can get." Did I take the advice to heart, thank him genuinely, and apply this new life lesson? Hell no. This is a book about failure. Instead of handling it like an adult, I muttered sarcastically under my breath (pissed off at what I perceived to be disrespect), "Hey, thanks for the tip," before sauntering away.

Big shot. I had all the answers.

From that point on, I became persona non grata in that precinct. I came to be the "Thanks for the tip" guy. For about the next six months, they made my life a living hell. They would screw things up in my locker, send me out walking miles on foot patrol only to call me "back to the house," saying that I forgot something, just to mess with me and make me walk longer and harder. They would squelch my radio traffic, so that I couldn't be heard over the air. I remember one night over the radio when I heard one of them snicker, "Thanks for the tip," after they iced me. I had completely failed to realize that what that older cop was trying to instill in me was the fact that you need social order to keep cops alive. You need young guys to understand that even the manual that we used could be interpreted in different ways and that you had to use common sense. I had to work my way back in to regain trust and faith. How did I do that? Simple. By dialing down my ego...*and shutting the fuck up*. Because nobody ever got in trouble for shutting the fuck up.

DAN BONGINO

I may have been book smart back then, but I wasn't street smart, as much as I may have believed that I was, from growing up in the streets myself. When you do something stupid, or make a decision that can eventually lead to people getting killed, you need to know about it. And I could never be mad at those cops for what they did to me because they taught me a good lesson. That failure more than paid off for me and, in turn, helped bolster the safety of my fellow officers.

Years later, when I was in the Secret Service, I took part in the New York State Police Olympics in upstate New York. I ran into the cop, Joe, who gave me that invaluable advice that night. I told him how much I appreciated what he did for me and how it brought me down to earth and helped ground me. How he helped stop me from believing in my own fairytale. He shook my hand, smiled, and told me that was just part of his job. Unfortunately, in the race we both ran, he tore a hamstring! I wound up with the silver medal. But to this day I remain thankful, and Joe, if you are reading this today, I will never forget what you did for me. I deserved it. Maybe even a little more than you guys hit me with.

As for the person who supposedly retaliated against me, that's the exact opposite of a good lesson. I did nothing deliberate to get her locked out of signing in. I had not exhibited any stupidity. The only lesson learned there was that sometimes people can try and get you killed, all thanks to a petty grievance. I got punished for doing nothing wrong, and so that's her failure, not mine. But hey, this is a book about failures. I didn't say they all had to be mine. And I sincerely hope that she eventually learned that she handled that situation the wrong way.

4

"The greatest glory in living lies not in never falling,
but in rising every time we fall."

—RALPH WALDO EMERSON

I learned some pretty serious lessons thanks to failure while working as a Secret Service agent. But before we get to the heavy stuff, I thought it might be fun to point out a few of the lighter stories (things that make me laugh today but probably should have made me cry at the time). Nothing life or death here, but the smaller conflicts and failures usually can teach you something quite important.

Up at Camp David, the president's retreat, there was a funny little incident that still makes me smile and think back about failure.

Something to understand about Camp David: first of all, while presidents may love this seclusion and privacy, for an agent, it's nothing to get that excited about. You're in the middle of nowhere, there's not much to do, and it's a rough place to try and sleep. Why is that? I'm not sure to this day. We agents used to joke that they were pumping anti-sleep chemicals into the little rooms we were assigned to. It was weird. All of us would wake up after just three or four hours of sleep, unable to get back into any kind of dream state. Everybody felt it. But we couldn't figure out why. Were they pumping in aerosolized adrenaline? Why the hell couldn't we get any decent shut-eye? First world problem? I have to be candid— it sounds kind of pathetic whining like this. But hey, it's a book about failure. I do like pointing out the human side of what it's like to be an agent. Unfiltered.

People think of Secret Service agents as a form of superhuman species that functions on its own wavelength. You see service guys all square-jawed, sunglasses on, detached from the world—I hope it's not a failure to reveal this, but agents are just people. You get up in the morning and you brush your teeth after a decent night's sleep. (But not at Camp David.)

When you are the new guy on the president's detail, like being new on any other job, you get tasked with the most basic grunt work, for instance when it's time to gas up the unmarked Secret Service tanks.

Most of you probably think that we have some special fuel resource when it's time to fill up, right? Maybe a mysterious, unmarked tanker that refuels us on the move. Or perhaps stealth underground reserves known only to the most exclusive and elite inner circle. The reality is *we go to freaking gas stations*. Just like you. We pull up, pull out the credit card, pop in the nozzle, stand there, and wait while the ads on those built-in TV screens blare away. Maybe cop a Slim Jim inside while we wait. (I'm a big fan of beef jerky.)

Another small failure (although not mine, this one belongs to the media): we don't refer to the presidential limo as "The Beast."

This is a media thing. It's what we call in law enforcement "buff talk." People who really love the military and the police want to use the jargon, but they don't understand what they are talking about. In this case, we didn't even have the limo, what the media calls "The Beast," we had the SUV that we called the "Camp David." Nothing more, nothing less. The media loves to create cute, clever little nicknames, but I never heard one of our guys refer to anything as "The Beast." It just doesn't happen. In fact, that term helps us delineate who knows what they are talking about and who doesn't.

There was a little gas station up there in the mountains, a couple of pumps, and a little Quik-E Mart attached to it. The guy that ran the place knew who we were, what we did, and who we were protecting. Not a big deal. He was used to the drill.

On this particular day, we gas up, and as we are driving away, I'm looking in the rearview mirror and I'm wondering to myself, why does it look like the suburban has a tail? (Hey, maybe the media was right, maybe it really was a beast!) Dragging behind us was this long black serpentine prosthetic, and then it hit me. My partner, we'll call him "Tony," had driven away with the nozzle still in the vehicle, and it broke off the hose and we were dragging it! I can already see the memes, had smartphones been ubiquitous back then. "You had one job. #Morons." We drove back down to the station. The owner could not have been any more gracious, and he told us that we were not the only ones to have done this. That hose snapped away because they had built in a failure mechanism for idiots like us who forgot to finish the job and replace the nozzle. We laughed it off, but that failure reminded me that life really is about the little details. Showing up to work on time. Making sure you don't smell. Speaking in complete sentences.

Remembering to put the nozzle back on the pump.

We were just men and women. Occasionally we made mistakes. But if we didn't learn quickly from those mistakes, we would've been out of a job. And lives could have been lost (along with a nozzle or two).

One of the best lessons from failure I learned right before that time was when I worked in the transportation section of the service. It was very heavy on the logistics. When I was new to the job, I was working in a satellite office out on Long Island. At that time, Hillary Clinton was running for Senate in New York. She would be out in my region a couple of times a week because Nassau and Suffolk counties were swing areas, and she was struggling a little bit in those places.

Ordinarily, new agents would never be given an advance assignment for the First Lady. But there was a senior agent in the office who was sick, therefore the pickings were slim. I was it. I wound up being the motorcade guy. It was a trial by fire for me.

So, I'm the young guy on the totem pole. All I know is what I learned in the academy. And I'm sure anybody reading this book can surmise that one day on the job is worth about three months in the academy in terms of experience. So, by relative standards, I don't know much.

Hillary Clinton is heading out to a wedding in the Hamptons. When most people think of the Hamptons, they picture high society, well-manicured lawns, and a very elite social scene. But that's only part of it. The Hamptons also has parts that are very much in the wild: rustic, unlit, untamed, and hard to navigate. This was especially true during a time when an atlas—that's right, folks, a paper atlas covered in plastic—was your primary source of locating someplace. Grid system. "A-6." "B-14." No Google Maps, no Waze, just an atlas and hopefully a good sense of direction. So I prepared. I went over the motor route four or five times, but the mistake I made was that I was using actual street signs as my location markers. It was just what I had written down on the spreadsheets, as I had learned in the academy. It didn't even occur to me that on game day, you don't have time to look at the signs. If that's all you're looking for, then you've already gone too far. They are too small. You need a primary visual landmark that you can see ahead of you that's not going to creep up on you. You have to call it out. The sign comes up too fast—so what are you going to do, bust a hard right or hard left? That's not going to work. You have a trail of cars behind you.

It was embarrassing. I was in the lead car with a Suffolk County detective from the Suffolk County Police Department, and we got lost. And so now, Hillary Clinton is going to be late for this wedding. Interestingly, when you're in the Secret Service and you get lost, nobody knows you are lost unless something happens. Usually, we have alternate routes and other built-in safeguards so that if you missed the turn, nobody would know. The problem for me on this night, however, was that she noticed a big barn at one point and commented on it. "Wow, look at that barn. It's so nice."

We wound up doing one huge circle. A few minutes after she commented on the barn—there it was again. It reminded me of that great scene from the movie *National Lampoon's European Vacation*. Chevy Chase gets caught in the traffic roundabout and says, "Hey look kids, there's Big Ben! There's Parliament!" Over and over again. So, we had a major problem. There was no hiding the fact that we didn't know where we were going or even where we were. Clinton's detail guy automatically called my boss to ask, "What the hell is going on?" but thankfully, the Suffolk County detective was a Hamptons guy. He figured out where we were and where we needed to go.

I had screwed up. I missed the turn. It was my fault. When you are protecting people's lives, there is no room for this kind of mistake. We wound up getting her to the wedding and everything worked out okay, but that was a close one for me. Again, small details are what determine the big moments in your life. But this was an epic failure of the first order. From that point on, I never considered doing a motorcade route without landmarks. I don't care if was the McDonald's arches or the Grand Teton mountain range. They don't teach you that in training. They teach you to "grid" it out and ride the route a lot.

I did multiple motorcade advances after that, and we never had that happen again. Some of them were in hot zones all over the world: Middle Eastern countries with terrorist problems, you name it. But I never had that issue again. And it's no use learning from failure if you don't pass it down to others, so I always use this lesson when talking to younger agents. I would tell them: I don't care what you learned in training. It's all about landmarks.

Later, I got yelled at by my boss, but I deserved it. He was kind of like my baseball coach, Coach Stan. No nonsense as it gets. He was an old salty New York City cop who had done the president's detail himself. He was a great guy, but he had a lot of pride. Having been on the detail himself, this mattered to him. He'd point his index finger at you and give you the "come here." So he let me have it, but I deserved it. I had let him down, and I felt terrible about that. He trusted me. By embarrassing myself, I also embarrassed him.

But at least nobody got hurt or killed.

So yes, we Secret Service agents get our own gas, map out our own routes, and focus on many small details that most people would probably think we are above doing. The lesson? Focus on the little stuff. Fail on the little stuff. You will never get the big stuff. Also, make sure you take those lessons you learn and pass those on to the ones behind you. Otherwise, what's the point of any of this? Never miss a teaching moment or those failures weren't worth anything.

Now, on to the bigger story.

5

"I do not fear failure."

—GENERAL GEORGE PATTON

The Secret Service has a tactical team called the Counter Assault Team, or CAT, and they are badass. They don't wear suits, they wear black battle dress uniforms (BDUs), and most of the guys that go into that group are my kind of guys: MMA (mixed martial arts) guys, Special Forces guys, workout guys—tough guys. My people. They're a little bit older, early thirties, and they may not make the best war fighters because of age. (For that you'd want twenty-year-olds in Delta Force and Navy SEALs.) But for CAT, the job description is different. The physical part obviously matters, but not as much.

CAT came about in 1979 when the Secret Service had an idea. Since the service role was to run, get out of the box, or get out of the hot zone, the brass knew that agents could be chased. So they created this heavy-weapons team to stay back and duke it out. That's the general operating principle that gave birth to CAT. They had the biggest, toughest agents. And it started as a branch of the president's detail.

Anyway, these guys are badasses, and the thing about the Secret Service is that we run. We are not there to duke it out. It's not a "measuring dicks" contest. If someone is shooting it out with the president, we're not there to shoot back. We run. And if we can't, we are the bullet magnets. It's not about cowardice; it's about saving the president's life—and if necessary, sacrificing yours in the process.

The way the president's detail works is that there are pre-satellite and satellite details. So you will spend likely four to five years in the Presidential Protective Division (PPD). There's a graduation of assignments with escalating levels of responsibility within the PPD.

The greatest assignment you can get on the president's detail is to be a "lead advance." Very few guys will get to that level on PPD. Look, very few get in the Secret Service, period. The same principles apply to CAT, where due to very rigorous fitness and shooting tests, very few make it there. And there are no exceptions. At least that's how it was back then before "woke" culture. I've been out of the Secret Service for a while. You either did the pull-ups with the enormous, weighted vest on, you ran the mile and a half in the allotted time, you did the push-ups, and you killed the paper targets with the proper scores to get on a CAT team, or you didn't. There were no discussions or brownie points. It was a pure meritocracy, and I think even the agents on the detail respected that. I know I did. There was a metric for success that you had to be aware of before going into a tryout for CAT. This is what you had to do. Period. There are no commas or semicolons. There's no excuse for failure here. This is the CAT physical fitness and shooting test. So if you don't know you can do it, then why are you even bothering? It's like being late for a train. What the hell is your excuse? The train comes at 8:05. How did you not figure this out? These are the kind of failures that bother me more than any others: the obviously preventable ones.

Now, why this story is relevant...

So you would get on the detail, and you would be assigned a shift. One of the working shifts protects the president. You would get all of the garbage assignments for the rookies. The garbage assignment is working with the press. Although you don't want anything to happen to anyone, if something happens to the press, it's far different than if it happens to the president. So they will throw the rookies with the press and that way if he screws something up, at least he won't get the president killed. That's just a hard reality. As a press guy, you watch the explosive ordnance disposal team and the canine team check the press's equipment for explosives. You observe that, and then you stay with them all day to make sure that they stay "clean." That's your job. Once the press's equipment is "swept," you just make sure that nothing is compromised throughout the rest of the day or night. The press is going to be with the president all day, so you need to check for bombs and other things. Your job is to babysit the press pool. You sit there basically and make sure that after their equipment is swept, nobody goes and puts a bomb in one of their camera bags. That's the job. So, nothing too hard.

Like everybody, that's where I started. Then you go to a pre-satellite detail. It's usually one of the children's detail. I was on Jenna Bush's detail. You spend maybe nine months or so on that detail. And again, obviously, you don't want anything to happen to that child. It's a much different threat level and a much different situation than if something happens to the president.

The service is trying to graduate you up in terms of responsibility. And through all of this, you get familiar with the PPD culture. It's not the same as the Secret Service culture.

It's like two completely different jobs. Imagine comparing an accountant to a firefighter. I mean it's that different. In one, you are doing criminal investigations in a nine to five setting. In the other one, you are rotating hours and one slip could get the president killed. Two completely different cultures. On the topic of failure, it's important because that is a zero-failure environment. Something happens in that environment, and the world can change. The history of humankind can change with these kinds of failures.

So that's the graduation process from being a shift agent mostly working with the press to a pre-satellite. And then you go to a satellite detail. Now, when the CAT team was created, that was one of the satellites. So the satellites you had to pick from were CAT or the First Lady's detail, FLD (that's where all the pretty boys would go—the guys with the slicked-back hair and the expensive suits). There were also counter surveillance units, or CSU, which honestly, not too many people liked because it's kind of like an undercover thing. It's like you are in the Secret Service, but you aren't. You're just roaming around the crowd looking for bad guys. But the assignment can get monotonous. Some people liked it, but not many. It was rarely anyone's first choice.

Then there's the Transportation Section, or TS. TS is where all the accountants go. Like, the killer accountants—the ones that have the ultimate killer instinct. Of all the satellites, TS is the absolute no-fail environment. If you get lost with the president in a motorcade, it's not only an international incident and embarrassment but you can also get him killed. Remember, every single asset you have—closing off a highway or a local road—every single asset you have is on that route. So if you get off the route, you're vulnerable, and you may get the guy killed.

I had always wanted to do CAT. I loved the black ninja suit. I was into jujitsu, boxing, and working out, and these guys just had a camaraderie. There's always been an esprit de corps in the Secret Service in general, but this was next level. The CAT guys had an extra degree of loyalty to each other. And they were expected to carry a "CAT coin" with them at all times. They have a coin they carry with them for the rest of their lives, everywhere. It's cool. If you ever see another CAT guy, you're supposed to challenge him about his coin.

It always reminded me of other zero-fail entities, like the US Marine Corps. When I was an instructor in the Secret Service academy, we'd get a lot of Marines who would come in as agents. I always respected the hell out of the guys. No matter what happened in their lives, they were always a Marine first. A guy can be the CEO of a Fortune 500 company. But he is still a Marine first and a CEO second.

I had always wanted to be a Marine myself. I was just about there, right at the brink, and then the NYPD called, and I opted for that. I always considered that a huge life failure, not becoming a Marine. I still do. So I always respected these guys. And CAT guys were like that. Once a CAT guy, always a CAT guy.

I wanted to be a CAT operator, so of course, Murphy's Law kicked in. I had everything figured out. I was an instructor in the Secret Service training center. I was in the operation section, known as OPS. In the Secret Service, OPS guys run everything. So even though it was just the training center, it wasn't truly "operational" (we were just instructing students). I was the OPS guy, so I had the run of the place. I got a note from my boss saying they were thinking of pulling CAT out of PPD.

What was happening was high-threat, high-risk protectees would come into town and the CAT guys would go and work their details too. To show you how important CAT was to this high-risk detail, you have to consider that it's not about politics at all. We can't care how bad these people are from terrible countries. The attitude of the Secret Service was and is that no matter how bad you are, you are not dying here. I remember when I first got on, the New York field office just wrapped up Pope John Paul's trip to St. Louis. A lot of the New York field office guys worked on that. So, I'm brand-new. It's literally my first day as an agent. I'm pinching myself. I can't believe I'm an agent. And that first day in the office I notice all of these folders with Pope John Paul's name on them. And I mentioned it to one of the other guys: "Wow, look at all of these folders." And he said, "You have no idea what goes into protecting the Pope." He joked, "There are a lot of Catholics in the world. You don't want him dying in your country." I had never really thought about that, but he had a good point. That was the first thing I heard on the job as a Secret Service agent, and I never forgot it.

So, CAT was starting to get pulled off of PPD missions a lot. In order to fix this problem, they wound up founding a separate section called Special Operations Division, or SOD, and they pulled CAT out altogether and placed them under SOD. Not only did they pull them out, but this was right as I was about to go onto the detail. Shittiest luck ever.

At the time, my boss, Kenny, said CAT was going to be classified as a protection assignment itself, and in the Secret Service, you can only do one protection assignment. That's it. You had to pick one or the other. And I'm thinking, what the hell? I came here to protect the president, not do OPS in the training center. And I certainly didn't enter the service to chase counterfeiters (although it was fun). I loved training the students too, but I was there *to protect the president*.

That said, I also needed to be part of CAT. I genuinely admired their camaraderie, their no-fail missions, and the fact that when the president needs help, he goes to the Secret Service, but when the Secret Service needs help, they go to CAT. I had been training for it, and I felt I was prepared and conditioned to pass all the tests. I'd been dreaming about it, and I was ready for it. So I was devastated after hearing the decision. I thought, this is going to be a catastrophic failure. Even more so because I was still living with the regret of never having entered the Marine Corps.

I had a Secret Service picture of a CAT team up on my wall as motivation, and I could always picture myself in that image. One of the guys in that image was my backup (a quasi-supervisory position) in New York when I first got hired. All of them bigger-than-life guys.

Clearly, for me at this point, it was a failure to plan because I probably could have gotten out of the training center sooner. If I only had pushed hard enough. But I was trying to play the nice guy. Other guys ahead of me had squeakier wheels than me, but I kept quiet about it. I was told what to do, and I did it. And when it was my time, it was my time.

So now I'm devastated. I wanted to do these two things, and I wanted to do them so badly: protect the president *and* be a part of CAT. Sometimes, the best advice comes from weird places. I wasn't expecting Kenny to have such sage advice on this matter. He was a TS guy on PPD, and he loved it. TS guys were called "wheelmen" and that was his thing. He'd say, "If you're not a wheelman, you're not a real PPD guy!" (By the way, Kenny had been an offensive lineman at Syracuse University. He looked every part an agent: six foot five, 250 pounds; when you say "built like a lineman," this is that guy.)

I thought his advice was going to be, "Go to PPD, be a wheelman. What are you, an idiot?"

But that's not what he said. He knew the CAT thing really mattered to me. So he said a line to me that has stuck with me to this day. When we are given a binary choice in life, we tend to think, what do we want more, right? But as it turns out, that's the wrong way to look at it. As Kenny said to me, "That's the dumbest way to look at it." He said, "Why not ask yourself, what can't you live *without*?" When he said that, the answer was just so incredibly obvious. And I never turned back. The answer was that I couldn't live without protecting the president. That's what I was there for. That's what I was going to do. And it gnawed at me forever. It did.

I had a great run. I wound up becoming a number one whip (the equivalent of a backup on a protection detail) on the Secret Service Presidential Protective Division over two presidencies. "Self-praise stinks," as my Aunt Jane used to say, but that's a really big deal. I wound up doing three foreign advances overseas. It's tough to get a domestic United States-based lead assignment for an agent. It depends on how much the president travels, and it depends on how many boxes you checked in your career to get to that point. Because it's truly a numbers game. So it's significant to get a domestic United States-based advance and to get a foreign advance. Probably less than 1 percent of guys will do multiples. I did, but again, it still gnawed at me forever—not doing CAT. And toward the end of the detail, it struck me. When you look back, maybe a failure isn't truly a failure. At least not of your own making. After all, I didn't pull CAT out of PPD. It wasn't my choice. Yet I paid a price for it. Regret. I had a feeling I would regret this for the rest of my life.

I'd see CAT guys coming to the Secret Service office at the White House, and it smelled like a failure to me. I would see a CAT guy, and I would stare at him and think, I wish that was me. Why didn't I do that? But what I had perceived after my five-year detail, what I had perceived as a catastrophic failure, was one of the best things to ever happen to me.

When I started doing lead advances in my last year of the president's detail, and then being one of the lead advance advisors and teaching other guys and doing multiple foreign advances, I learned so much about myself in those stressful situations. Because I was in charge of everything. With CAT, advances are hard. You have to go out. You have to look at a site.

You've got to be sure you've got all of the tactical parts of the president's visit buttoned up. It's a hard job, but the hard reality is that when you are a lead advance, you don't just do the CAT advance. You have to know *everything*. You have to know the CAT guys; you have to see the tactical ingress and egress; you have to see everything. Where would the bad guys come in and out of? Where would they hide? What is the motorcade guy up to? Is this the best motorcade route? What are the FLD guys doing? Do they have de-confliction exercises going? What does the air picture look like? Do we have subterranean security underneath the street? (In case there are tunnels down there.) You have to see it all. I will never take anything away from the work those amazing guys do at CAT, but as I was doing lead advances, I started to realize I was better suited to this role. Managing. Delegating. Making mistakes. Learning from those mistakes. Passing that body of experience down to the next set of agents. I like the BHAGs that they taught me in business school: *big hairy audacious goals.* And I don't think I would have thought as big and hairy had I just done CAT.

So I had always viewed this as a failure. I missed out on the Marine Corps. I missed out on CAT. But I became a man on the president's detail. That's the win. That's the gift.

And the gift of failure is sometimes only matched by the gift of time. This lesson took years to learn. It wasn't quick and simple. You've just got to hang in sometimes and let the lesson unfold.

One thing I have learned is that when the failures aren't black-and-white and there's lots of gray, maybe take a breather. Get some time to figure it out. I thought I had it all figured out. Even though I wanted to carry that CAT coin for the rest of my life, it didn't happen. Life isn't always what you want it to be.

And there's more than one kind of superhero.

I think another quick lesson is that even if you do consider it a failure (like I initially did), don't judge the moment too quickly. I initially regretted it so much. I really did—my first year on the pre-satellite, I'm watching Jenna Bush eating in a restaurant in Argentina, thinking to myself, *What the hell am I doing here?* Nothing personal. She was great. She treated us well and I hope we reciprocated. But I would think, *Why here? I could be on CAT.*

Another lesson is: when you get caught in a situation like this where you feel like you made the wrong decision or have taken the wrong path and there's not an immediate availability for a course correction (which there wasn't—I was on PPD, locked in for five years), make the best of it and keep looking ahead to where it might lead. Don't get weighted down obsessing over what wasn't, but rather look toward what *could be*. I put my heart and soul into it and even though I may have regretted sitting there watching Jenna eat brunch in Argentina, I gave 100 percent, and it did turn out to be an incredible experience.

6

"You cannot fail unless you quit."

—ABRAHAM LINCOLN

The biggest advance I ever did in the Secret Service and the one I learned a ton from was Barack Obama's 2010 trip to Indonesia.

He had spent a good portion of his childhood there, so this was a very critical trip for him personally and politically, with lots of ramifications. Regardless of my obvious political differences with Obama, of course, I was going to do my best to make sure the trip came off flawlessly. I was honored that I got picked. I think outside of doing the Afghanistan advance in a war zone for Obama (that was probably the most dangerous trip), this one was viewed by the other agents as *the* trip to get. It was a big deal. It meant a lot to the Obama family. They weren't going to pick a bunch of tomato cans to do this advance mission.

Everybody who got picked was A-team level, even the airport guys. The airport guys are the newest agents, and it's the easiest thing to do. (That's because airports are the easiest ways into a country. You're not going to swim! There's a template. It's been done so many times; all you've got to do is call the last guy and ask him about it.) But even *they* were specially handpicked. It was like The Avengers. I was flattered to be asked to do the lead because I had already done a foreign lead advance. To do a domestic lead advance is a huge deal. You have to go to school for it. You have to train for it. To do a foreign lead advance is a whole other thing. You're dealing with everything from international diplomacy to a different language, to an expat population, to different law enforcement and military cultures. These are all variables that don't play in the United States. I had done one already so the fact that they didn't give it to somebody else was amazing.

I knew the Indonesia trip was going to be high stress, with lots riding on it. I was well aware of that. So I headed off to Indonesia to do the advance with an extra sense of focus and determination.

If you have not been, there's probably not a more difficult mid-to-large-sized country to get to than Indonesia. If you were to drill a line through the earth from where I was, you would be on the other side of the planet. And that's where I was heading.

I used to joke that there was a guy in my neighborhood who wasn't too bright and I told him I was going to Indonesia. He was trying to make the argument to me that a fifteen-hour time difference is worse than a twelve-hour time difference (Indonesia was twelve hours). I still talk about this on the radio. The worst time change in the world is twelve hours—because then you start coming back in the other direction! It doesn't get worse after twelve hours; it starts getting better! Would a twenty-four-hour time change be difficult? Of course not. Logic, people, logic.

Indonesia is simply a very hard trip. You're talking about a week and a half of acclimation to the time change and everything else. People often get sick in foreign countries, and so on.

So, I take the flights over. Longest I've ever been on planes. Six hours to Los Angeles. Five-hour layover. Sixteen hours to Japan. Another six-hour layover, then to Jakarta. It's like a nightmare trip. So when I get on the ground in Indonesia with my team, I'm a zombie and I can barely function. Walking dead. When we hit the ground, I load up on caffeine and get to it. The Indonesian people could not have been nicer. That country had been through a lot, and I appreciated their good nature. I got to the first meeting with the Indonesian support staff, and they could see I was practically falling asleep because I was so tired, but they were cool.

I'm there with the military, the staff, and my Secret Service team and I notice the Indonesians are not talking to the staff guy much at all. We are describing what the president is going to do and they keep looking at me, so I say to my counterpart in the Indonesian military, "Why aren't they talking to the staff guy? He's going to coordinate the trip; I'm just going to handle the security." And he said to me, "They listen to the guys who have the guns. The guys who have the guns have the power."

And it hit me, being a citizen of the United States, he wanted to deal with me. We had the power. The staff guy was okay with everything. It was fine, and we eventually smoothed things out. But it was just interesting to me.

So we had our meeting, then my Indonesian military counter-parts wanted me to go out that night to grab some adult sodas. It was considered the ritual thing that you do out of respect, like the post-work culture in Japan. I've now been up, with just a few brief respites of napping, for upwards of thirty-six hours. And I was starting to wonder if everything was real, or if this was some kind of *Matrix* scenario. That's how delusional I was getting. Thank-fully, my Indonesian counterpart, Frega, noticed my eyeballs rolling back into my head. He laughed and said, "We will get you back to the hotel early."

And I could not have been any more appreciative. So even though I was wiped out, I went out with them. My body was physically ready to break. But then they eventually brought me back to the hotel and all was well.

So, the stress is mounting on the trip. The president wants to go to every place, including Kalibata Heroes Cemetery, which is like their Arlington National Cemetery. It's a very intense advance that we are doing, and the whole place is a security nightmare. I'm watching TV each night and I see terrorists are getting whacked while we are there, all through the areas where we are going to be.

I'd look at my Indonesian security counterpart and say, "Did you guys have anything to do with that?" He would answer, "Don't ask questions you don't want the answers to."

I continued to ask questions. Just not about that.

We worked hard for two weeks, and the trip was basically done. Very little sleep. I was existing almost exclusively on this jerk chicken dish—breakfast, lunch, and dinner. I smelled like a jerk chicken store because I was just sweating out the cumin so intensely.

I hadn't worked out or done much else, so I wasn't feeling great, but then the craziest thing happened: they were taking a sudden vote on Obamacare, and we got word the trip was canceled.

The Indonesian guy I had been dealing with said, "I can't tell my president they're not coming." I said, "Listen, I had nothing to do with it. I don't know what to tell you. If I could call Obama's cellphone I would, but I can't." And after Obama canceled, they were pissed. And the Indonesians wanted my head on a platter like I did it. Talk about a failure.

We shook hands and were as cordial as we could be, but it was awkward. It was a major embarrassment, but I just glossed over it as best I could, expressed deep apologies, and then headed home.

It took me maybe a week to reacclimate. I'd lost weight, and my body clock was all off since I was still on Indonesian time, I'm back at work at my regular job but hey, that's the job. I get it.

A few weeks later, I got a call. "You have to come in and talk to us. Obama is going back to Indonesia." Are they kidding me? I had just reacclimated. It was now a hostile environment since we had canceled once. Now I've got to go back?

I said, "Why not give it to somebody else?" I had been there two weeks; the advance was completely done, and the schedule would be the same. "Just give it to someone else. They can check that box, say they did a foreign advance, and I did all the work." But the boss said, "No, you are going. You are doing it."

So here we went again. Six hours to LA. Japan.

Melatonin time.

Only this time we were flying through Frankfurt, Germany. During the layover there, I got a call that—wait for it—there had been a massive oil spill in the Gulf of Mexico. The BP Deepwater Horizon spill. *Trip canceled.* Can you believe that? I had to call the Indonesian guy again and pull the plug. Thankfully, I had not hit the ground there yet, but it was still a tough call to make. If I thought they were ready to kill me the first time, now they were ready for a public hanging.

A nice lady at the airport saw that me and the two advance team members I had with me were beyond exhausted. We were on the phone with the special agent travel office trying to figure out how to get back. We'd been flying all night, and so this lady in Germany upgraded us to first class. We each had our own little room and everything. Very nice of her. I never have forgotten the lady from Lufthansa.

Then I woke up back at Dulles Airport.

So back home, I acclimated one more time, back to work, and then I get a call. You know where this is headed. "Hey, Dan. You're going back to Indonesia."

"You're screwing with me, right?" I said. Nope. Real deal. I told them this time it really had to go to someone else. Not a chance, they told me. I was doing it. No discussion. "You are doing this trip whether you like it or not." I said, "One condition. I'm picking my own crew. I want ringers. We're going back for the third time? I'm the bad guy in Indonesia? Every terrorist knows we are coming back. I want the best. The A-team of A-teams."

And they said okay.

It was rare on these trips that I would ever say goodbye to my wife and kids and think we were going to get killed. But this was different. I seriously thought I may not make it back.

"Honey, if I don't make it back, it's been great!" Fifty-fifty shot of getting home? If we were lucky! That's where my head was at. (As I was sitting writing this particular part of the story, I looked over at Paula and asked her if she ever thought there was a chance I would not make it home. She shook her head, "No." Always my source of strength.)

So, I picked my rock star team, even the airport guys. I picked *superstar* airport guys. Everybody was overqualified for this trip.

And...everything went shockingly well.

I was expecting all kinds of static from the Indonesians, but it didn't happen. They couldn't have been more professional. Full success with the trip. Not. One. Hitch.

But of course, that's not the end of the story. We finished the trip and were getting ready to go home. Just as we were about to get out of Indonesia, a volcano eruption occurred. Obama had managed to get out. He was gone, but we were stuck. All flights were getting canceled. I was trashed after months of this project. Cells in my body were waving white flags. "Uncle!" But guys have got to get home. I sat with the logistics guy ("Tony," the guy who left the gas nozzle in the SUV at Camp David!) all night to make sure the security team could get out safely. We were stuck in this hot zone, with no protection, every terrorist knew where we were, and a volcano is going off...are you kidding me? But we did it.

We were able to finally fly guys out but had to use the worst routes home you could imagine, some with five or six legs through many countries and states; however we could, we got them home. The special agent's travel office lady was sweating blood to do this, but we finally did it. Me and "Tony" were the last two guys. I wasn't going to leave him alone. And finally, we all got home.

When it comes to failures, this was a repeated failure to launch. But there was something important I learned. If you view these things as multiple-trial learning rather than a single episode of failure, then it becomes *a positive*.

What I had perceived as a big disaster for my career—an epic waste of time and waste of opportunity, something that *should* have been a screwed-up trip—wound up great. In the end, I came to believe, as I do today, that we got the job done not despite the failures to launch, but *because of the failures to launch*. Had I not gone through those two false starts, I don't think I would have known how to truly operate in that country. I wouldn't have had the contacts that I wound up having. I would not have known how to fully manage my foreign support teams. With each failure, my abilities became stronger. Those multiple failures forced me to learn the ropes and do a better job. They made me more of an expert. They made me more prepared. In the end, even a volcano couldn't screw things up. I was ready for anything at that point. My big takeaway from the entire Indonesian episode was that failures to launch aren't really failures at all. They become powerful practice runs that prepare you for the future.

7

"Never confuse a single defeat with a final defeat."

—F. SCOTT FITZGERALD

I was sitting in my living room with my wife. It's 2007, and we lived in Severna Park, Maryland at the time. I'm about two years in working on the presidential detail, and this is considered the gold standard of Secret Servicing. If you're on the president's detail, you're like a small group of gods. (One of the funny things I remember was a small poster that we would give out during recruiting. It said, "You elect 'em, we protect 'em.") There's a myth out there with the *In the Line of Fire* crowd (the famous Clint Eastwood Secret Service movie). People who saw that movie think that *everybody* in the Secret Service protects the president. In reality, very few people in the Secret Service do. It's just not the way it works. It's a small portion that does that. It's highly competitive to get in, but thankfully, I made the cut.

So, I'm in my second year on *"the"* detail as we call it (Secret Service insiders, you know what I mean), and things are going pretty well. I've done some good quality, low-level advances, and

I've gotten great feedback from my bosses and supervisors and most importantly from fellow agents, whose feedback I thought mattered the most. They were the guys doing the work. I'm feeling good.

But I was sitting on this cheap chaise lounge we had in our living room (we didn't have a lot of money, so we couldn't afford anything too nice), and my wife was watching that TV show *Grey's Anatomy*. She loved that show, and so we'd watch it together when I was home. Now, if you know me, I'm a doer. George W. Bush used to say of himself, "I'm a doer. I do stuff." (We'll leave the politics of what he did for another book!) Well, I'm a doer too. That's me. I just do stuff. I don't overthink anything and sometimes obviously it has resulted in failure (hence this book), but hey, doers understand that risk is a huge part of the reward. An agent friend I looked up to, Steve, used to repeat a paraphrased quote to me from Matthew 19:21, "The heavens have a way of putting a price on things." That always stuck with me. The risk is the price. And we are restless. I can't just sit on my ass when there is downtime. I have to be doing something.

I'm a product of what I grew up around. As I recounted in my first book, there was a guy who worked his way into my family's life, a genuinely tough guy who was only scared of one thing, and that was the cops. We had an incident one night that frightened me as a young kid. I went from red-line panic around this guy, to serenity when the cops showed up. Then I knew everything would be okay. I had no idea how that one moment would affect the trajectory of my whole life.

Something else that had affected me: the old *Charlie Brown's 'Cyclopedia*. They had them at the supermarket on Long Island, and my mom used to bring them home for me. In that beautifully illustrated fifteen-volume set, there was a book about the human body. And it mesmerized me. You know, "This is your body. These are muscles. This is a skeleton, and this is what a cell looks like." That was huge to me. I think to this day I am so obsessed with working out because of that book. Thanks to that book, I just became so fascinated by this awesome machine that God gave us. (Thanks to modern technology, I was recently able to track down the entire set, which I proudly own today.)

And...it made me want to be a doctor.

I like fixing things. So, what better thing to fix than the body? So I turned to Paula on this particular night in front of the TV and said, "I think I want to try and get into medical school."

I was already done with more than half of my Secret Service education, with most of the hard parts finished. She sat up in surprise. Even knowing me, she had to think that this seemed over the top. "Uhm, this is not the kind of thing you just, like, decide while watching *Grey's Anatomy* on the couch."

And I was like, "Normal people don't, but I do."

"I think you better kind of think this thing through," she said.

"I have. While watching *Grey's Anatomy*. I want to go to medical school."

And that's how it started. That's just how it started. She said, "How are you gonna do that? You've been out of school for a long time."

Doers don't usually respond well to reason. In my head I was thinking, I have done a lot of graduate work in neuropsychology. So at least from the neck up, I felt like I had a pretty good background. But from the neck down, I had only taken my biology classes in my freshman year of college. And I had graduated decades earlier.

No big deal. I said to her, "I think I can do this. I'll just go buy some textbooks and figure it out myself. I'm gonna go back to school." She thought it was the craziest idea she'd ever heard. "You're going to teach yourself physics and biology all over again? And organic chemistry?"

I said, "I can do it. Me. Doer."

Here's the deal. We had a saying in the Secret Service: "Hurry up and wait." For a job that was as stressful and busy as it was, there was a *lot* of downtime. (Some background: We protected dignitaries and the president. They are not moving around 24/7. And there's a rotation to keep people fresh. Stale eyeballs are a protection agent's worst enemy. You stare at things for fifteen to thirty minutes; you get into a zone. We just joke and call it "Ring around the Oval." So when the president is in the office all day, there's a series of posts. And you just keep rotating posts. One-two-three-four down. Repeat. So it becomes monotonous after a while.)

I'm not a time-wasting guy. As a matter of fact, I *hate* wasting time. I said to Paula, "I guarantee you, with all the downtime, I can study for the MCAT" (Medical College Admission Test). So I bought a bunch of chemistry and biology textbooks. Then went out and bought the Barron's prep book for the MCAT. I think I memorized every question in the book. I must have read that Barron's book ten times, and I spent a good year just plowing away and just really reteaching myself. The organic chemistry gave me a hard time. That's the kind of thing, even if you have a professional tutor, it's hard to learn. I did my best on that, but the other stuff came back really fast, and I didn't have a difficult time with it.

So I busted my ass for a year. Keep in mind, the whole time, I'm assuming I'm going to get in. I'm putting in hours and hours each day for this. I was essentially a full-time student while being an agent. So I'm thinking to myself the entire time, this is going to go my way. Look, for a guy who some think comes off as fired up and pessimistic on the radio (I get it), I'm not like that at all. I'm a super optimist (and I'm long on the United States). I just had this crazy idea that I was gonna get into medical school and *that* got me through. Positive spirit. Not easy but I still did it. I'm busting my ass, our friends are out drinking and partying, and I'm glued to this freaking Barron's book. But failure was not an option. My friend Kenny, the linebacker-like Secret Service agent, used to say, "Don't let the evil in." So I just never let the evil in. I just always thought I was going to get in (and by evil, I mean doubt). So I studied and I busted my ass for a whole year.

And what happened?

I did well on the MCAT. I think I got a ten on the biology. Pretty good, not great, but certainly good enough (I thought). Better than the median. I applied to the University of Oklahoma because my brother-in-law was a doctor within their system. I figured I had a good chance because he could write a recommendation for me. I got all the way up to the end of the process and...they took a bunch of in-state people.

I was rejected. *Total failure.*

Hard to relive this moment even as I write this now. I can feel the disappointment creeping back in. Everything drops. Stomach, lungs, and throat. You feel the failure all over. I had never considered not getting in. Done deal, right? Wrong. I studied the entire year and got nothing. That's right, nothing. I'm not gonna BS you and say, "Oh, I learned about work ethic." Bullshit. I'm not going to sugarcoat this. That's not me. I didn't teach myself a work ethic. I already *had* the work ethic. I had done the work, and I had failed. So what did I learn? Sometimes, work ethic leads to nothing. This was a failure—a blunt, full-force failure. I'm not going to give you any flowery psychobabble about the positives of this sort of a bust. This is not that book.

I saw no bright side. There was no, "Oh, I got in later on in the next round and became a surgical assistant and made millions!" It was just a dead end. Did I get a little bit smarter about science? Maybe. But so what? (I do have to say I was really good at *Jeopardy* after all of this.)

I was reeling for a few months. Devastated. Doers hate to fail. A year of my life. Gone.

It was a pivotal moment.

When you fail, you don't fail alone. Especially when you are married to someone who is living it with you. The ups and the downs. Everything. So this was a tough time for Paula and me. Things were tough. We were struggling a bit. The Secret Service was wearing me down. We had a young child. Paula herself was working hard. A lot was going on in our lives. And in this case, she became the doer because she had to pull me out of the doldrums. I will never forget that. Paula not only has a maternal instinct but also a spousal instinct where she knows how to step in and take care of everything.

After a few months, as I typically always do, once I got up off the mat, I started walking around and surveying the landscape again. I said to myself, "All right, well this is a failure." And I never knew I was gonna write this book in the future, but I kept thinking of this line from one of my really jacked friends, a guy who looked better than anyone in the gym but who had very shitty genetics. He said this: "What's my secret? Well, everybody goes to the gym when they feel like working out. It's the guy who goes to the gym when he *doesn't feel like it*. That's the guy who looks like this."

And I thought, that's me. After getting your ass kicked and studying for a year and getting nothing out of it, most people would just sit there and dwell on the failure. I thought, I'm not gonna be that guy. I'm gonna go to the gym when I don't want to. Maybe I don't want to do anything right now. Maybe I just wanna feel bad for myself. But that's not an option.

So, I started looking at other things. Law school? Well, I figured studying for the LSAT (Law School Admission Test) was gonna be another year, and I was getting old. I didn't have time. So I had to make a compromise. And you know what? Moral compromises are a part of life. (Modern-day cancel culture specialists could learn a lot from that prior sentence.)

I didn't want to study for another year. I had no time and besides, I had a family, and my wife was getting a bit exasperated. She had married me as an agent. She always knew I was a dreamer, but I knew I was becoming a handful. She didn't marry a doctor in training. So all of a sudden, I was giving her "life whiplash."

But I had to do something.

I thought about business school. I like business. As for the GMAT (Graduate Management Admissions Test), I figured, how hard can that be? I just studied for the MCAT, the gold standard of aptitude and achievement tests. I'll get a book, I'll study for a few weeks, and then boom, I'll ace it.

Happy ending time, right? Guess again. I pretty much bombed on the GMAT. I did not prepare as I should have, and that is all on me. I got cocky and scored terribly as a result. But this time I was ready to fight. I was still determined to make something happen. I was now motivated to turn a failure around.

So, I applied to Penn State. A professor in charge of new student intake called me, and he was confused because I had a really good GPA in graduate school, like 3.8 or so. I was a Secret Service agent who had a pretty good resume. "How the hell did you screw up the GMAT so bad?" he asked me. I was not gonna try and bullshit the guy. I told him what had happened with the MCAT, how hard I had worked—that I knew how to put the time in. I urged him to take a flyer on me—in other words, take a gamble. And I convinced him. So I think part of the lesson in recovering from failure is that a lot of this stuff is pure luck. (Remember that luck isn't pure; it's a product of chance. And the more chances you take, the better your luck may be. Simple arithmetic.)

This guy took a flyer on me. He believed in my passion and conviction. But he told me, "You screw up one semester, your ass is out of here." And I said, "Fair enough." Yeah, it's not "luck" that helped me sell myself to him. But let's not kid each other. If he had not been in the right mood that day, things could have been very different. A little luck never hurts.

As it turned out, I graduated toward the top of the class. There was no luck there. Just a lot of hard work. And a lot of juggling. And a lot of patience at home. Ambition can have some negative side effects, especially to those around you. Those can represent failures of their own that need to be dealt with. The point of this story is that a big medical school failure resulted in my taking a path that ultimately had a profound effect on my life. I may still inside always want to be a doctor. But I would never trade that for what I have become as a businessman. Not a perfect businessman. You will soon learn about plenty of failures that I have experienced in business. But that's okay. As I hope you're starting to see, those failures, redefined, can start looking like the big, brightly wrapped presents that they are.

If I fail to remind you of that, then I am failing as an author.

8

"If you fail to plan, you are planning to fail."

—BENJAMIN FRANKLIN

When I think about failure, it's hard not to think about politics. A few of the biggest failures in my life are directly related to me attempting to win public office. And political failures are some of the most devastating because they are so public by their very nature. But like everything else in this book, time and context matter most of all.

So how did it all start? Why did I first throw my hat in the ring as a candidate?

I had an interesting perspective as a Secret Service agent. I saw it all. Politicians, entertainers, athletes…everyone wants to be around the people with power. Sports and entertainment—they all commingled with politics, and I had a front-row seat. I remember doing an event for Bill Bradley when he was running for president. Most of you probably remember him as a star on those New York Knicks teams from the 1970s. Well, when he ran for president, he came out to Long Island to do an event, and I was assigned at that point to the Melville resident office, which covered Long Island. I couldn't believe all of the local power players that came out to see him. It was even more dramatic with the Clintons. Political people are magnets for entertainers and Secret Service agents are in the thick of it all. You get to see all the ass-kissing up close and personal.

I also got to see the behavior and machinations of politicians from the inside. When politicians would walk over to the West Wing from the East Wing of the White House, they had to go through this portico by the Rose Garden. I noticed that some of these Congress people would not wear their pins, which identified them as a member of Congress. I asked one of my coworkers, who had been on the detail for a while, why some of these people did not wear their pins. He told me, "They just want you to stop them, so they can tell you who they are." I couldn't believe that. That got in my head: that these people would act like such tools. The arrogance. That stuck with me. These were people that were elected by American citizens, who were supposed to be "representatives" (it's their actual title!), and they were playing games like this? It was all about ego and power. It had very little to do with serving the people. Talk about a failure. Maybe that's one of the design failures of our government: that being an elected representative has become such a draw because of the power and the influence, that the actual job of governing and representing the people is a distant second.

Similar to that *Grey's Anatomy* moment, which I described in an earlier story, when I found myself impulsively deciding to go to medical school, this moment under the portico also had an important effect on me. I thought to myself, I've got to do something about this. I need to get involved. I know it sounds corny and probably a little hokey (and there's nothing I hate more than hokey), but I thought I could do it differently (probably naïve on my part, but some things you just can't help).

When I told Paula what I was thinking, it didn't throw her for a loop. She understands me better than anyone. What was funny, however, was that my Aunt Jane, my godmother, was staying in our house at the time I was contemplating this monumental decision. She had come down to visit for the holidays. She heard me and Paula talking about this, and she couldn't believe how casual and even cavalier my suggestion was about running for office. I told my aunt, "Paula and I have a funny way of talking to each other. We finish each other sentences. It's not a big deal to us." But my aunt was blown away. The fact that I could throw out something so life changing and just have my better half not freak out, admittedly, had to look strange.

I understand that to anybody watching this scene or even to you, the reader, learning about it right now, it may seem a little bit crazy. Who leaves the job in the middle of their career to run for office and talks about it like they are headed to a kid's party at Chuck E. Cheese? But that's just how my mind works. Remember, I am a doer.

Paula had questions, for sure. She said to me, "Look, you are halfway done with your career. You finished the president's detail. You are in the Baltimore field office, which is a really hard office to get in the Secret Service."

My commute was twenty minutes. The field office was not too small and not too big. Everyone was friendly. The workload was just right. I had it all. Paula added, "You have worked so hard to get here. You realize if you walk out that door, that's it. There's a good possibility we won't have anything." She was working at the time but even that was about to come to an end. So it was a crazy idea. None of it made sense. Not the finances, not the career development, nothing professionally or personally, but doers just sometimes do stuff on a hunch.

While Paula was entertaining this thing, my aunt was thinking, this guy must be a lunatic. I just didn't know what I was going to do next. I was searching, thinking about how I could make a difference in the world. And Paula got that.

She was right. I had worked hard, I had put the time in, and I was in a good place professionally. If I decided to make this move, all of that job security would vanish. No more benefits, no more regular salary, just a headfirst dive into one of the most unpredictable existences known to man:

Becoming a political candidate.

I kept bothering Paula about it for five or six months. I just had this bug. I had to do something bigger. I had always been a conservative with libertarian leanings.

After months of my lobbying, Paula finally said, "If you really want this, I will support you. We will do this."

Two weird peas in a weirdo pod. That's just us.

While working at the Baltimore field office, our team had broken up a major fraud ring, and I was the case agent. Interestingly, it resulted in my first appearance on a major radio station. I was interviewed on WBAL (the big talk radio station in Baltimore) about the case while I was still an agent. This was such a huge deal to me. Me, on the radio? I fell in love with the experience. It was a chance to be heard. Some recognition in the public eye. Others may lie to you and say that this stuff doesn't matter. But I'm not going to do that. I just thought it was very cool, the entire experience. It was only about ten minutes on the air, but I fell in love with it. Never nervous. I just enjoyed the whole experience. The energy of the studio was something very special. When that "on air" light goes on in a studio, it's like you've entered an alternate dimension.

Our case was also on the cover of the *Baltimore Sun* newspaper. This was getting fun. When you're an agent, accustomed to being behind the camera and not in front of it, these are big moments.

Now, Maryland is an unbelievably blue state and there was a US Senate race going on. When Paula finally said, "If you're going to do it, you might as well do it," I was taken aback a bit. Usually, people run for smaller things: dog catcher, school board…you get your feet wet. To go right for the Senate was a big deal. You need money. You need access to media. You need access to emails and volunteers. I had none of those things. And in the DC market, nothing is cheap. To win that race in a blue state, one was probably looking at raising and spending about $15 million and even with that, your chances were slim.

It was illogical. But I could not let it go, and Paula knew that. I had none of this figured out. Nothing beyond the feeling that I simply had to do it. It wasn't as if I had not accomplished anything yet in my life. I had done many things that had a purpose. As a New York City cop and a Secret Service agent, I felt like I had made significant contributions to changing people's lives. It's hard to describe. I just needed something different. There was a sense of fulfillment of a purpose, and I was so confused as to what that purpose was.

I'm not suggesting that this was some brilliant idea. I had no idea what was going to happen. But I knew I wanted to do it. So when Paula asked one last time, "You're never going to let this go, are you?" And I said, "Probably not." She said, "Okay, I think you should just do it."

That was it. When the coach tells you to get in the game, you don't respond, "Who me?" You just get out there.

As I write this right now, it's hard not to think, was that a failure? Being too impulsive? Succumbing to a whim? Not properly planning? And was I getting in over my head when there were other opportunities more suited for my "height"? It's kind of like when you go to a theme park, and you are not quite ready for the big boy rides.

I contacted Tim, my first-line supervisor in the Baltimore field office, and told him that I needed to talk to him. I think he thought it was about the fraud case that was still going on.

I sat down with Tim and said, "I think I'm going to resign." The look on his face was one I can't even describe. Confusion? Shock? Am I being punk'd? I think he was wondering if I was mentally stable. I had a great promotion in store. I had just done the most complicated part of my career, the PPD. I was resigning at the peak of my career. But then I told him what I was resigning for. "I'm going to run for a Senate seat here in Maryland." Now I was thinking they were ready to call somebody in to give me a psych analysis. He said, "What? That's the craziest thing I've ever heard." It took some time to convince him that this was not a joke. That I was serious. He was flabbergasted. I don't think his eyebrows came down once. And that was it. I gave my two weeks' notice. An internal announcement was made, and over the course of a couple of weeks, I started getting all of the emails from people I worked with. I had to keep stressing to everyone, "Yes, I am fully aware of what I am doing. I have not lost my mind." I mean, at least I didn't think so.

But then it occurred to me that people who lose their minds never think so. So how would you know if you really were?

Looking back on what the true motivation may have been, I'm still not completely clear. I'm sure in some other books, they give you a retrospective analysis of their lives, and they've got it all figured out. I don't. My wife and I still wonder how we did what we did.

But I have a close relationship with God. I've prayed since I was a kid. When you're a sinner like me, you have to. It's a very close relationship. I feel like we know each other. I remember begging God for my mom and dad to get back together. That's how the relationship started. I always felt like I was supposed to do something different and that God would guide me in the right direction. Again, I had done so many meaningful things as a cop and while working on the president's detail. I just had this profound feeling that it was time for something different. I was ready for a change. I felt that as a politician, maybe I could leave the earth in a much better place than I found it. I was just stepping up from where I was. It was all vague. But still real.

I had become friendly with a guy named Brian Murphy who had run for governor in Maryland. He had gotten Sarah Palin's endorsement, which was gold back then. He didn't win but for a newcomer, he did okay. For me, it was amateur hour, I had nothing, so I reached out to him for advice. I knew so little. I said to him, "Do you have an email list for some media people?" And he gave me five or six emails, and I just went online and searched for everyone else in the local media market that I could get a hold of. Paula knew what she was doing technology-wise, so she built the initial list of people we would start reaching out to. We had no money. I mean, *zero* money.

So we started a campaign, and I managed to get on the ballot. In our small dining room, we typed up the email announcement that I was going to run for Senate on Paula's computer. We added the email addresses of the only people we could dig up on the internet. We looked at each other before hitting the "send" button. Paula's eyes said to me, you have one last chance to bail out of this. But her mouth said something different. "You sure you want to do this?" And with my right index finger, I hit the button. There was no turning back now.

Remember the line I mentioned earlier? What we would use in recruiting Secret Service agents? "You elect them; we protect them"? Well, I was on the "elect them" side now. I was on the ticket with ten other people, and we launched an email campaign because we had nothing else. Early on, I was not good at messaging, but I had a feeling it would make waves that an Obama Secret Service agent was running for office as a Republican. I thought if I got lucky, I might get another appearance on WBAL. But this time it would be about politics, and not a criminal case. I never thought it would become a national story.

Within a week or so, a booker from Fox News called and asked, "Is this story real?" They called Karla, who was volunteering with me. I'd love to say she was "handling the press," but because we had nobody else, she was the jack-of-all-trades: campaign manager, wrangler, everything. And she was a pit bull. She believed in me, and she was as tenacious as any media person I've met to this day. They couldn't believe the story was real. It sounded crazy to them, and she said, "Yes, it's real. It's definitely real," and I was invited on to the Neil Cavuto show on Fox. I had done one interview on the radio again with WBAL, but this time I was kind of nervous because I was on there as a politician. I wasn't sure what I was doing, sitting in my basement on a cell phone thinking it was going to lose signal.

But this was TV. (TV is much different, a lesson I learned in a huge way later when I got my own TV show.)

I had been around media at the national level, essentially for the last five years of my life while traveling around with the president. And yet it was strange being the guest and not the protection agent. It was a different kind of excitement. It was like the opposite of the Secret Service. It was a fear of the unknown. Whereas, in the Secret Service, you better not be fearing the unknown. You better know the known! So this was a different experience. Neil could not have been any nicer. I went up to New York, and he made me feel right at home. The interview went unbelievably well. Anytime you can fit a Thomas Sowell quote in, I think it would usually go well, especially for a primarily conservative audience. I walked off the set on cloud nine. Everybody was texting me right afterward. I must've received one hundred texts and emails complimenting my appearance. Now it was getting real.

I just had to pretend facts and logic didn't matter. I was probably upwards of a ten thousand to one underdog. And that may be generous. But onward regardless. So we did an event at my friend Brian's house. He was a very smart guy and close friend, and he and his wife Kristie put on a fundraiser, which went pretty well, though I was thinking, you all might as well flush your money down the toilet at this point. But my neighbors were nice. They all showed up and I think we raised $9,000 or so. (Interestingly, Brian was so inspired by the fundraiser and my foray into politics that he later decided to run as a state delegate. He lost by a sliver in his first race, but he would eventually win— all because of that event!)

Not long after, I was invited back to Fox News to be on Gregg Jarrett's show.

Unfortunately, that interview didn't go as well. I'm not sure why. I think I was tired, and I just wasn't ready for interaction that morning. (Come to think of it, that's pretty much every morning. Which is why Paula wound up buying me an espresso machine.) I also did the show *Fox & Friends* while I was there, which went a little bit better. I thought maybe it was over after the Jarrett interview but, shockingly, more money started coming in, and volunteers too.

Nobody of any significance had declared yet. That would change later, but for now, it was just me and a couple of perennial candidates. So I essentially had the Maryland political room to myself on the Republican side. How was I getting the word out? The only way I could afford to: for free. I was out there waving signs at Baltimore Ravens football games, for one. It was embarrassing. I would sit there in the walkway with my signs and say hello to people. What better way to get name ID, a key component in politics, than to talk to potentially seventy thousand people for free? I would go to Redskins games and do the same. I saw the looks on people's faces. The overwhelming majority would be thinking, who is this crazy guy? Which I learned to ignore. I would be crazy to pay attention to it because it gets in your head. I would also wave signs at bridges and intersections, and it made a difference (even my podcast producer today told me recently that the first time he ever saw me, he was coming over the Bay Bridge from Eastern Maryland, and I was there waving a sign).

Well, now things started to gain some real momentum. We had a few dollars, which meant we could start paying Karla. She had, by now, become a total beast with the media. She would call anybody and everybody: every network, every local station, every newspaper. She would get under people's skin, but the big break finally came after her repeated attempts to get me on Sean Hannity's radio show. She had gotten the number for Lynda, who has worked for Sean forever. Karla was haunting her to death, calling her practically every day, and finally, I got a call from Karla. She said, "You are never going to believe this. Hannity wants to have you on his radio show." "No way," I said. But it was true. I was connected with Lynda who told me, "Karla is the most persistent woman ever. I'm not doing *you* a favor by booking you. I'm doing *myself* a favor just to get her off my back." There's a germ of truth to every joke. Simple life lesson there: persistence. The sale is only over when you stop asking.

This was a huge score, all thanks to Karla. Sometimes you have to put your pride on the back burner and just go for it. You don't want to go over the red line where it becomes creepy, but you can go right up to that line sometimes. Karla had turned that sensibility into an art form. So I did the radio show with Sean, and it went amazingly well. My best one yet. I was comfortable, I found a groove, and I knew why I was there. Also, Sean made me feel like I belonged.

I wasn't going to be Teddy Kennedy; a guy who blew his 1980 presidential run by fumbling a big media interview, which then basically killed his campaign. I was prepared with good, strong answers. I knew what I wanted to do, and explained how I felt that as a society, we were becoming a kleptocracy and an oligarchy. I was a legitimate outsider, but I had seen the inner sanctum. I had worked in the White House for years, so I knew what was going on. That made me unique.

THE GIFT OF FAILURE

I got a call right after this interview from Karla saying, "They want you on Hannity's TV show tonight!" So I took a seat on the "Great American Panel." I jumped on the Amtrak Acela and headed to New York for the most exciting train ride of my life. I could not believe I was going to be on that show. I arrived at Penn Station and walked up to the Fox studios, getting more excited with each block that I crossed. This was different than anything else I had done there. This was prime time. Thankfully, the show went great. It was fun, it was relaxing, and I felt like I had done a good job. On the way back on the train, I looked at my phone. I had a processing system for donations where I would get an email each time something came in. That would drive a more experienced candidate crazy, getting an email every time somebody contributed. We had so few donors, however, that I thought it was cool to get every update. And then I would call every low-dollar donor and thank them personally. Somebody would donate five or ten bucks; they would get a call from me. This was more than just "grassroots efforts." These were the roots *under* the grassroots. I did this for a while until it became impractical when many more donations started coming in.

So, I was on the train going home from Penn Station in New York and donations were pouring in—probably $10,000 over the next couple of days, which for me was a huge deal. That's what blasted the doors open.

We built some more momentum, and then finally a serious competitor entered the race: Richard Douglas, a defense department official. Now, we had a dog fight on our hands. Primary night came around, and I was expecting to lose. In a race like that where we had spent no money on ads, it's such a long shot, but... we pulled it out. I defeated William Capps, Rick Hoover, Joseph

Alexander, Robert Broadus, David Jones, Brian Vaeth, Richard Douglas, John Kimble, and Corrogan Vaughn in the Republican primary on April 3, 2012.

I was thinking, holy shit. My first time out of the chute, and I'm the GOP nominee for the US Senate. This was the craziest thing. It was a big deal. I felt like I had made it. Like I had proven myself. On primary night, the feeling was total elation. Then I started thinking, maybe we have a shot. Pro tip: we didn't.

After I won the primary, I started booking regular media appearances, and a lot more money started coming in. Once we got over $1 million, we could start to get some things done: buy some ads and pay people. You know, act like a real campaign.

We were building some momentum, and I felt like we might have a chance against the incumbent, Democrat Ben Cardin. Michael Steele, former Republican lieutenant governor (and resident Republican basher on MSNBC), ran against Cardin before me and by Maryland standards, he did well. In a book about failure, it's important to realize that sometimes, winning can be losing. I was running to win, but a side of me thought that if I could ding this guy up and do better than Steele did as a newcomer, then I was going to position myself to change Maryland politics and send a message to the machine. I would, at a minimum, collapse that margin.

And who knew, maybe we could catch lightning in a bottle and even win. The Tea Party was happening. Things felt like they might be lining up.

And then...*boom*. A third-party guy came in, Rob Sobhani, this super wealthy guy who entered the race and spent more than all of us. He spent seven or eight million dollars of his own money and sucked all of the air out of the room. I wound up getting eviscerated. Sobhani got about 17 percent of the vote. Now, I was just happy to beat him. You don't want to come in third place in a race like that, being a major party nominee. But of course, the media narrative became "Dan Bongino gets one of the lowest percentages of the Republican vote in Maryland history." That was tough. I even wrote a rebuttal to one of the Washington newspapers pointing out the fact that they conveniently left out how this guy spent more than both of us and that I still beat him.

Regardless, I went from what I thought would be, at a minimum, sending a message that we were serious, to dealing with a triage operation. Sometimes a good defeat can be a victory in that it sets you up for later. But this wasn't that. Now I was just worried about a horrible defeat with nothing to show for it. Failure on many levels.

I had built a lot of name recognition, but so what? Charles Manson has name ID as well. It doesn't necessarily translate into something good.

Like with what happened with medical school, I came out with a goose egg. So there I was. A big, shiny new failure to deal with. A lot of pressure: kids to raise, mouths to feed.

But as I'm sure you can now sense, the theme developing is that failure also comes bearing potential gifts. You just have to be patient. Problem is, I'm not the most patient guy.

Should I use this failure to stick with politics and apply what I had just learned over the last grueling months?

That was the big question.

9

"Don't fear failure—not failure, but low aim is the crime. In great attempts, it is glorious even to fail."

—BRUCE LEE

Election night was a devastating experience. Winning the primary had been incredible. But on that winning primary night, the impossible nature of what was ahead had not hit me: a first-time candidate, with no significant fundraising, so no shot of winning the Senate race. That was the prevailing attitude.

Primary night I thought, this isn't too bad. I've beaten nine other people. My father was proud of me that night. He was there. He's a more practical guy than me, very methodical. He reminds me of a drill sergeant, and I mean that respectfully. He gets up at 4 a.m., writes down his to-do list, and that's what's going to happen the rest of the day. He had been skeptical of my decision to run. My grandparents were very risk averse. For them, if you had a government job, that was gold. You would never give that up. It was a Depression-era mentality that carried down, so my dad was skeptical when I jumped into the race. When we won that night, seeing his reaction, it was an emotional reward for me. There's nothing like making a father proud.

Once I won the primary, it had not hit me that I had probably less than a 1 percent chance of winning. So I just enjoyed that moment. It was one of those nights you say to yourself, I want to wake up in the morning, but if I don't, I could go out like this.

I was learning that in politics, you have to lie to yourself a little bit (or in this case, a lot). You have to tell yourself that *anything* is possible. Even when you know it isn't. I thought maybe I had some special political gift that people would respond to and help override the massive political chasm. *Make* them vote for me. I don't mean in the liberal way, like dead people in the cemetery. I mean like the power of persuasion. I was out there in the pouring rain, the freezing cold, knocking on doors. At train stations, I tried to greet everyone who passed by. People were laughing at me at Ravens games, Orioles games…as I waved to them. It was a lot of work. I did all of that because I lied to myself. I thought I had some profound political gift, and maybe I did, but political tribalism is hard to overcome. Reality is a beast.

So you know, I don't like being around groups of people in public. I'm almost clinically antisocial when I'm in public. Very low-key. I don't initiate many conversations. I like people, but I'm just not that social. So becoming a politician was counterintuitive. If you're not a social person, getting into politics is the most asinine thing on planet earth. Parents tell you two things: (1) don't ask people for money and (2) don't talk about yourself. That's all politics is. And I was uncomfortable in both of those respects.

But I had to do it (or I'd fail!).

I can't tell you how many chicken dinners I went to by myself in Maryland. (Political fundraisers are known for chicken dinners.

It's the cheapest way to raise money. And everything tastes like chicken.) Nobody had any idea who I was. After I won the primary, maybe a few people knew me now, but hardly anybody. It was embarrassing. "Hi, I'm Dan Bongino running for Senate!" "Leave me alone...I'm eating, and it tastes like chicken."

You get used to that rejection after you run for office. You'll talk to anybody about anything. Your fear of social situations feels surgically removed. You get rejected so many times that it's character building. Your skin gets thick, like burlap.

It's very hard to succeed in the world without a sense of interconnectedness. It was a personal failure for me to be that way, and politics helped me overcome it.

So, it's finally election night and you think to yourself, anything can happen. When in reality, no, not everything can happen. Maybe it happens once in twenty-five thousand races. And you ain't it. It was deep blue Maryland after all.

It was the year of Mitt Romney/Barack Obama—a tough one for any Republican candidate.

We were at a hotel in the heart of Maryland by BWI airport. We had a big ballroom on election night and a bunch of people showed up. Everybody knew I would lose, but I was impressed that the people showed up anyway. It was like going to a funeral for someone who had lived a really good life. And even though I knew I was going to lose, I was still busting my ass right until the end. You owe it to everyone who supported you. Let's go out on top; let's give it our best—that was my attitude.

I was thinking of something to say at the end of the night. It's hard to give a speech when you get smoked. What do you say? "We almost got 'em?" Well, we didn't. There was a guy, Andrew B., a donor of mine. Good guy. Very wealthy and worked his way up. Not a trust fund kid. He called me that day he said, "The only thing you can say tonight is," quoting 2 Timothy 4:7–8 (NIV), "I finished the race." It was true. I took it to the limit. I went the distance.

It wasn't the most devastating feeling in the world. As I learned later, in politics if you're going to lose, get smoked. Get absolutely crushed. I know it sounds counterintuitive but think about it. You'll never say to yourself, what if I had just knocked on a few more doors? We got crushed, and it wasn't as hard as I thought it would be because I thought to myself, all right, if we had knocked on one thousand more doors it would not have mattered.

That night, Paula was looking at me as if to say, "What is plan B?" She loves me and had put in a lot of work. She was patient. But we had no healthcare; we had nothing because the COBRA insurance plan we had was going to run out.

What was plan B? I didn't have one. The night ended, and I did not have a plan B. Or a plan C. Or any other letter in the alphabet. Remember, this is a book about failure. And failures rarely come with backup plans.

I spent lots of time thinking of what to do. I started getting invited to speak by a few national conservative groups. People found me to be a bit of a curiosity. Why would I run in a blue state like that? I had made a bit of a name for myself. I'd become a decent public speaker by then, so I gave a few speeches that seemed to go well, but I was still relatively directionless.

A few months later, I started thinking, maybe I should give it another shot. I was thinking about a run to be the governor of Maryland. I thought, if I'm gonna go for it, I'm gonna go for it. The governor was Martin O'Malley, and the guy was a total disaster. He thought it was a good idea to "tax the rain." The tax was to be levied on impervious surfaces: driveways, parking lots, and other hard surfaces that do not absorb water. Republicans, who in Maryland can be kind of feckless, got smart and branded it a "rain tax." If you want to piss off Marylanders who have a lot of flat roofs, just start taxing the rain. It was a disaster for him and a brilliant piece of branding by conservatives. It worked.

O'Malley's lieutenant governor, Anthony Brown, decided to run, and I started thinking, I can beat this guy. I had taken some informal polls, and I felt good about running for governor.

My then-deputy campaign manager, Kelly, analyzed my numbers, and she came back and said, "Even though you got smoked in the Senate race, it was a three-party race with a well-funded independent. And you did well. There's optimism here." So I'm thinking, I'll run for governor. We started a little "whisper campaign" to plant the seeds and the internal numbers started looking even better for us.

Kelly came back to me soon after and said, "If you look at these numbers in this district in western Maryland, I think you have an even better chance of winning the congressional race in District Six."

I wanted to run for governor, but I let them "data watch" me out of my gut instinct. Failure on my part. My gut said, "Go for governor," but I let them talk me out of it. Politics and data can be great, but sometimes you just have to stick with your gut.

I didn't, and it's still one of the biggest regrets of my life right up there with not going into the Marine Corps. That was something I always wanted to do. And I let my mom talk me out of it because her brother, my uncle, was killed in Vietnam. Understandably, she was never the same after that. I had been offered the NYPD job and that was that. So she thought it was destiny that I not go in the Marines.

It was also a big mistake for me to shift course because the guy who wound up winning, Larry Hogan, was a weak, sniveling little guy. He called me one day, begging me to get out of the race. I think he knew that based on our grassroots support we would win. But I didn't get out because of him. I was listening to my team. Hogan went on to win an enormous upset, despite being poorly funded, and a generally awful candidate, begging us for volunteers to close out his campaign.

So, I jumped into the congressional race.

Running for Congress was different than running for Senate. We could feel something happening during this race. The first time out, we worried too much about bullshit things. What matters are votes. We had cute little signs in the Senate campaign that nobody could even read. So for this race, we made everything a bright, obnoxious yellow. We marched in a parade, and people saw the ugliest shirts ever. We were like a swarm of bumblebees.

But make no mistake, nobody forgot who we were.

We felt momentum. It even has a name in politics. They call it the "Big Mo." Via a lot of small donors, we raised a good amount of money. We had lots of volunteers. So many so, that it created a problem for me.

I desperately wanted all of them to feel special, because they were doing something nice for me. But as a campaign grows, it becomes more impersonal. And that always hurt my feelings. I always wanted to make it special for them. As a matter of fact, the first guy to ever show up for a race at all for me, was a guy by the name of Brian King. It was for a parade in Baltimore for the

Senate race. And I told him I would never forget that. Brian, if you are reading this, now you know that it's true.

But back to the story…

I was running against John Delaney, one of the richest guys in Congress. We were told we had zero shot, but I was feeling something different. I saw the momentum. I felt it in the streets. The Tea Party rebellion had long since started, and for the first time, I wasn't lying to myself when I said we can win this thing.

That said, one of the worst things that can happen in politics is when you start to believe your own bullshit and hype—and I was starting to. And I did that. People were seeing all of my volunteers, hearing me all over national radio, and I was even filling in as a guest host on some prominent programs. I was all over the place. And I finally had the thing craved most in politics: name recognition. Remember the line Al Pacino utters in the movie *Donnie Brasco*, playing "Lefty"? "I'm *known*. Forget about it." That was me. All of a sudden, I was "known."

Forget about it.

So yeah, again, I started believing my own bullshit. I started getting radio show offers, but I still thought I could win. Do we bail? What do we do? I thought about it to myself and wound up taking a two-week break while I deliberated over one specific radio job offer. And that hurt us. That two-week breather was brutal. Eventually, I turned the job down and then went back to banging on the doors, hustling for votes (unlike Pacino's "Lefty," who was hustling diamonds).

And as unlikely as it all seemed, I still felt like *maybe* we had a shot.

Shortly before Election Day, I got a call from a newspaper, I believe it was the *New York Times*. This reporter said, "I want to talk to you about your congressional race." I'm thinking, why? They had never shown any interest in me before. But we were desperate at that point for any coverage, so I took the call. He said, "Your opponent just dumped hundreds of thousands of dollars into an ad buy. That's odd, don't you think?" And it was. No political pundit had our race on any radar; they thought it was a fait accompli for the Democrats. "Why do you think he did that?" the reporter asked. I had no clue. Us? We had run out of money. But obviously, the other campaign was sensing something.

The night of the election, we were at our hotel ballroom, and since I couldn't imagine winning, I was writing my concession speech on a napkin (which I still have). My buddy Brian, a cop friend I went to the police academy with, was there with us in Montgomery County at the hotel. His phone was the only one getting good internet service. He came up to me when the first county came in and said we were down by about ten points. So I kept writing my concession speech. I was resigned to losing. Everyone was kind of down in the room. Then, about fifteen minutes later, Brian tapped me on the shoulder and said, "Look! You are only down seven." Interesting. As people were starting to get faster internet service, I got more reports. "You're down five... three...WTF, you're ahead!"

Holy shit, I was winning. The energy in the room went off the charts. My mother-in-law, who comes from Colombia, an immigrant who came here with nothing, said in her thick accent, "I can't believe you're going to win this. I'm so proud of you!" My father could not believe it. It was crazy. I was getting emails from all over. I was ahead for about two hours. The whole room was going nuts.

The night went on and then one of our data analysts started to see trends, and it started to get ugly. We had to win a sliver of this one overwhelmingly Democrat county, and it didn't happen. Eventually, we lost the race by a nose. A couple of thousand votes. But they didn't call it right away. It was too tight. They called the race officially by Friday. As I said earlier, big losses are easier to deal with. Just over one point? I was devastated. To use an over-used cliché, it was like letting the air out of the balloon.

Losing by such a small margin, I thought to myself, what if I had not taken those two weeks off? I think I would've won. Major failure on my part. Those two thousand additional doors I could've knocked on. Again, if you're going to lose, get destroyed. It's just easier.

Making matters worse was learning from an activist group that a large number of people that had voted in my election declared on their jury duty forms that they weren't citizens. But what could I do? It would have been a hard and expensive fight to challenge it. And the odds were stacked against us to win. I was ready to move on.

Of all the failures of my life, this loss was one of the low points.

We had two daughters at this point and I now, again, had no plan B. Or C.

I had turned down the radio job. I had suffered an apocalyptic failure. And I had no idea what the future now held. We lost by a hair. I couldn't close the deal. Hogan was the new guy in Maryland, and it was time for me to move on. Sometimes the greatest gift of all is having nothing to lose. That's the gift of this failure in that moment.

I was sitting at home for weeks saying, "What am I going to do?"

A blue state loss like that the second time in a row was my clue to hang up politics in Maryland. Two second-place finishes? So what.

"Close" only counts in horseshoes and hand grenades.

For the next few weeks, I had a lot of time in my hands and that can be a dangerous thing. Especially for me.

I was sitting at home reading an article and doing some homework about how the car radio was becoming a dinosaur. It described how kids were all digital now, plugging in their phones, and how this new podcast medium was being born. But back then the standard-bearer was still radio. Podcasts were for people who couldn't get radio shows. Adam Carolla was the only one getting any traction with a podcast.

I said to Paula, "Everybody's making fun of podcasters. That's where it's going—à la carte, on demand. I'm sure of it." I asked her, "Do we have ten thousand dollars?" She said, "No, but we have a credit card," I decided right then that I was going to get equipment and start a podcast. And that's how it started. I'm a doer. And I launched my future from my most apocalyptic failure.

It took two years. I got paid nothing for it, but I had no other option. Opportunities are born out of profound desperation. That's the gift of failure.

10

"Try and fail, but don't fail to try."

—JOHN QUINCY ADAMS

What happened with my last political run is similar to the previous medical school chapter. The Florida congressional race was just a straight up, nothing-good-comes-out-of-it failure. Nothing redeeming.

Well, almost. I'll explain...

Everything happened so fast. Remember, I had not moved to Florida to run for office, but rather so that Paula could be near her mother, on the east side of the state. I can't say it enough. If I had moved to run for office, why would I move to the wrong coast?

I had been down there a few months, and I heard a rumor that Rep. Curt Clawson was going to be leaving office. I had done some radio guest hosting on the west coast of Florida, but I didn't know the local politics that well. I got a call, and someone said, "Even though that's not technically your home, you've got good name ID over there. It's worth taking a look at." So I got a place over there and figured I'd dive in. And it didn't take a lot of convincing.

Remember, I'm a doer. I figured it was a short race, a few months before the primary. I thought, okay, maybe this is one last shot at the title. We hadn't been on the East Coast that long. We hadn't even been in Florida for that long. It was a quick relocation and in the realm of stupid decision-making (and poor planning), this sits near the top.

It was all just so poorly thought out. I jump into a lot of things I probably shouldn't, and this was one of them. There was hubris and arrogance at play here; I'm not going to bullshit you. I thought I had a decent name ID, and I was very confident. I thought that was enough. I was doing well on the speaking circuit. I thought I could be a walkaway winner with the right amount of elbow grease and door knocking. I wish I could tell you that there was more detailed planning, but that was it.

Of course, I'm going to pull it out, I kept telling myself. I was getting great responses to my speeches. It was a short sprint. In the initial name ID department, I had a leg up on everybody, so this race would be over quickly.

What I'm about to say sounds ridiculous and almost counterintuitive, but it's true. When you have a known profile due to national television and radio appearances, you probably have a better shot at winning primaries in a presidential race than you do in a local race. And the reason is quite simple. Running ads to get national name ID is expensive. But to get name ID in a local race isn't that hard. You can knock on doors, you can wave a bunch of signs...so one failure was thinking that national ID meant something, but it didn't. Appearing on Fox News all the time didn't mean I was going to win a local election. Not that I wasn't planning on working hard. I was. I just placed way too much stock on those national media appearances.

Well, I was right about that at least.

(I was still doing the podcast, by the way. The audience was still growing, but we had to limit ads, because I was running for office. But I still felt like I had an obligation to keep doing the show, so I stuck it out—I didn't wanna give up on my audience and let them down.)

A guy by the name of Francis Rooney entered the race. Very wealthy guy. It's that kind of money where he never looks at a bank account, ever. The kind of guy that probably doesn't need ATMs in his life. He was a prominent Republican donor and a former ambassador to the Holy See. He gave his campaign *a lot of money* and spent heavily on TV and mail. There were many older people in the district who still read their mail, and so that in particular helped him out. It was smart.

Chauncey Goss also entered the primary. He was a well-known Lee County Republican and son of former CIA director Porter Goss, who once represented the area.

It was a nasty primary. We fought a lot. Given my "Queens personality" and the more gentlemanly personalities of Rooney and Goss, we just didn't gel well. It got pretty cringy backstage at the debates, like oil and water, and I was the odd guy out. In the end, Rooney received 53 percent of the vote, Goss came in second with 30 percent, and I brought up the rear with just 17 percent of the vote.

Money can be overcome. It wasn't that which hurt me most. The other two candidates were better than I originally gave them credit for. They knew the local issues better than I did. In that area of Florida, local water issues take precedence over any political party. These guys both knew the water issue better. That said, I became my own worst enemy.

A reporter called me about a story that was getting some attention, but the story itself was bullshit. It presumed that I lived outside of the district, but I had a place on the West Coast. I had a place in the district. The reporter also asked me about having a paucity of local donors, and the narrative was that it was all big, outside money supporting me from my national audience. Again, bullshit. And it was easily refutable. Most of my local donors contributed small amounts, and anything under $200 was invisible. Those donations don't appear in public documents. But nobody asked hard questions or did any real research. (Sounds kind of like the current media environment now, right?) It was all easy to debunk, and we would have shown them our records had they just asked. We offered to give the reporter the information, but it didn't matter. They just ran with the story. So now I'm the "out-of-towner carpetbagger, with no local support."

That's what set the stage for me to become my own worst enemy. Or so I thought. A reporter from Politico, Marc Caputo, called me one day to comment on all of those things. It was adversarial from the moment I heard his voice. I knew the call would go south fast. He didn't like me, I didn't like him, and so I did what I do best sometimes—I just went volcanic. I cursed him out and well, that was the end of that campaign. The story was all over the place—me ripping this guy a new asshole. I was stunned we ended up getting even the 17 percent that we did.

We got crushed and remember, in politics it's better to get crushed than to lose at the wire. Then you don't feel like you left anything on the table. I closed the condo on the West Coast, and drove back to the East Coast, never to return to it again under those circumstances. It paralleled how I was feeling about politics.

Not only was the condo on the West Coast closed, but the political doors closed as well. It was a metaphor. I was done with politics.

It was a failure. But it showed me that political office was *probably* not for me. Activism? Yes. Entrepreneurship? Yes. But not politics.

I just don't like bullshit, and I don't like bullshitting people, and that's running for political office.

This is where the story takes a turn for the better. The strangest thing about that blowup with the guy, although he recorded me and I didn't know it at the time he was recording me, was that I think people saw the real me. Yes, I let him have it, but what kind of "reporter" addresses a subject like this: "So let's see, you move down to Florida from Maryland after losing two campaigns in Maryland. You say you were going to stay in Maryland and fight. You run away to Florida. You go look to run in District Eighteen. You see you're not gonna be able to win there. You try and run in District Nineteen. You are losing there. You're like a professional political candidate who loses, Dan. You just lose. Oh Dan, why are you yelling? Oh Dan, you really sound like you need some help. You realize you sound like you need medication. Do you need some professional help?"

Me blasting him back was the real me. It's not my most flattering moment, but you should listen to it because that's me.

Look, you fuck with me, I'm gonna fuck with you back. That's who I am. In the political world, that kind of attitude is a problem, but in the real world, where things matter, people like people like me who don't take any shit. It's something that I feel is important to point out. If you hear that interview with me and Marc, I want you to know that that same guy—who at the time seemed so belligerent and confrontational—when I came down with cancer, sent me a nice note expressing heartfelt concern for my condition. It was a nice reminder that no matter how intense things might get with your adversaries, there are more important things than politics. I'm not suggesting he and I are going to go out for beers together. He's a reporter. And I'm always taking shots at reporters. I had it in for this guy because at the time I thought he cost me something special. I completely appreciated what he did when I got sick though because it also reminded me how much negative energy can eat up in your life. At a certain point, you have to let go and simply accept a thoughtful gesture from a decent person.

The podcast started to go crazy after that happened. After that blowup, the audience just exploded and I thought to myself, this isn't so bad. People would write me and say, "You tell it like it is." Now, I don't know what "it" is but whatever it is, I seem to tell it. Some sort of je ne sais quoi.

If the Parler/Rumble episodes were the genesis of my personal activist autonomy, then the fight with this reporter was the genesis of my career as a podcaster. It may not have been pretty, but it was real. It was pure frustration and anger at a machine that far too often manipulates and dishonestly deploys false tactics to try and destroy people whose political narratives they disagree with. The people spoke when it came to the election, but they also spoke when it came to reacting to how I handled this guy. Again, not my finest moment, but what resonated more than the anger and profanity was the very real fight against forces that were conspiring to destroy me. And, by default, you. So I will take that. I will own it. And I'm guessing I might even do it again.

11

*"Success is stumbling from failure to failure
with no loss of enthusiasm."*

—WINSTON S. CHURCHILL

Failure can come in many different shapes and forms. Sometimes we are responsible for it, and sometimes it's just randomly thrown in your face. Either way, you have to deal with it and hopefully come away with something informed, productive, and positive.

At least I do.

In August 2020, Donald Trump accepted the Republican nomination for the presidency for the second time at the White House, and it was a big night. Because of the pandemic, a large stage was set up on the south grounds, and thus the nominating event was held not at an arena, but at the "People's House." Paula and I were proud to have been invited. We talked about it for the entire week leading up to the event.

It was always interesting to go back to the White House, even though I had not been an agent for about ten years. I couldn't help but watch all of the newer agents on duty and think about what they were going through. I'd watch the guys standing in the same place for hours, and I'd at least want to go up and get them a bottle of water. Or I would have loved to stand post for them for a few minutes and take the weight off their leather-soled shoes. But I'm pretty sure the Secret Service regulations prohibit the agents from turning their weapons over to civilians regardless of prior experience. Once you walk out the door, it's over. What can I say, once an agent...always an agent.

The atmosphere was electric and also quite dramatic. David Dorn, a seventy-seven-year-old retired black police captain who had been fatally shot after interrupting the burglary of a pawn shop in The Ville, St. Louis, was honored in a touching tribute by his wife. President Trump poignantly paid tribute to the fallen hero, and it was quite moving. There wasn't a dry eye in the house. There was also much pageantry leading up to a massive fireworks celebration, which helped trumpet his Republican nomination. However, the loud explosions from the pyrotechnics covered up the sounds of what was happening outside of the White House on the streets of Washington, DC. I just told you moments ago: once an agent, always an agent. But I guess that was a failure because an agent would have paid attention to what was going on outside. Full-scale riots had broken out courtesy of the cowardly Antifa and BLM chumps, similar to other events that had been wreaking havoc all across our country during that long, hot summer. Paula and I only got a sense of it as the final smoke from the fireworks settled, and it was time to leave. If you listened closely, you could hear it. It was hard to tell exactly the severity of what was happening, but it was clear that something resembling chaotic pandemonium was raging out there.

At the end of an event like that, the Secret Service has to quickly clear everybody off the White House property. Remember, they are there to protect the president, not you. I used to know this. It didn't matter what was happening out on the streets. They had a job to do, and they were doing it swiftly and effectively. They don't fool around because they don't have that luxury.

The closer we got to the west side gates, the more I had a strong sense of how dangerous it was out there. Now you could hear it: the screams, threats, and even their own fireworks. I asked one of the agents if we could exit on the east side of the White House because our hotel was right there. But they told us no, everybody had to leave on the west side. Remember, it's all about the boss, the president, not you. On a normal night, all of the streets would've been open, and things would have been easy to navigate. But that was not this night. Many of the streets and arteries were closed due to what was happening with the rioters, and so all of a sudden, our less-than-quarter-mile walk was going to be several times that because we had to loop out far and wide due to the closures.

The moment we hit the streets outside the west gate, I knew we were in trouble. To this day, it's hard to describe. I had been on many a tough ride before as a police officer and had seen tons of chaos as an agent, but there seems to be this weird invisible shield around you when you are working. You're focused on everyone else's security. You're not processing it as a "bad situation." You're processing it as a problem to be solved. So I never saw it that way. But this was now, and things had changed. Suffice it to say, it was an incredible security failure in the city that night. The Washington, DC, officials in charge at the time should still be embarrassed.

This was a massive failure obviously, and myself and many others to this day are horrified by what happened.

Just steps from the White House gate, Paula and I were accosted by the Antifa and BLM crazies. Seething, raging, and blind with hate, they came at us, screaming that they were going to rape Paula, among other horrific threats.

The entire scene reminded me of a *Mad Max* movie. It was an otherworldly, Third World train wreck that did not even seem like America. It was like Pablo Escobar's Colombia. People were salivating and rabid. "We're going to rape your wife!" they kept screaming. I hate tough-guy stories. Most people who talk about fighting are the ones who are most afraid of doing it. Also, I have a temper. One of these guys lunged at me and my wife. I honestly don't think he was going to do anything. I think it was one of those, "I'm going to lunge at you and you are going to lurch back because you are scared of me." But then when he psychologically recognized that not only was I not scared, but I was actually going to lunge at him, all of a sudden, the dynamics instantly changed. Massive failure on his part. He saw that I wanted more. And Paula knew it because nobody knows me better than her. So she grabbed my right wrist, and said, "Boo…" (she calls me that sometimes) "please, don't." She pulled my right arm once more and then I realized that because she was in heels, I would have hurt her and not the guy because she would have fallen. So I reluctantly stopped. For me, the failure to act was a good thing.

There were two older Asian women on the corner who were crying, scared beyond belief. They came up to my wife looking for help and said, "We just need to be safe." A couple of border patrol guys (who I recognized as regulars on Fox News) stepped in to escort them away to safety. They also walked us back to the hotel. Power in numbers. That's not some special secret security rule that I learned when I was an agent. It's just a matter of fundamental truth in the animal kingdom. I don't know what would've happened to those ladies if we hadn't grabbed those guys and gotten them help. And I'm glad we did.

This was the first time that I got kicked in the teeth with reality. You can work riots as a police officer. You can watch riots on TV and know they are real. But it's different when you're "in the suck" (an expression we used to use in the Secret Service) and you become the victim (and you can see their hair and smell their breath and see their spit). They made a point to terrorize anybody walking down that street, picking out random targets at will. Paula was terrified. It was the first time I'd seen her really scared. It was just a matter of luck that nobody recognized me because that would've escalated things, I'm sure. I shot video on my phone because I wanted evidence to show people what the end of the world looks like. What it looks like when the crazies win. And they won that day and night in Washington, DC.

They don't know your politics. They just want to scare the hell out of you. I did not anticipate the mayor of DC allowing this to happen. Something allowed these people to get to this point where they felt it was okay to terrorize innocent people. Then again, the left has always deployed "shock troops" to shut down the opposition in the streets, or in this case, simply anybody that got in their way.

Eventually, Paula and I safely made it back to our hotel, but it was touch and go. We were exhausted more from the stress of the walk than the walk itself.

What was the gift of this massive failure? On a personal level, I was reminded of the value of restraint. Had I lost it and gotten

2002 Police
Olympics
referenced
in the book.

Presidential
Inauguration for
President Barack
Obama in 2009.

First Fox News
appearance in
2011 on the Neil
Cavuto show.

DANIEL BONGINO (R-MD)
US SENATE CANDIDATE

Second appearance on Fox News, which didn't go as good as the first.

Campaigning for the US Senate in the middle of Baltimore City, 2012.

Sign-waving in Prince George's county in the middle of the rain with Brandon, one of our most dedicated volunteers.

Dundalk Fourth of July Parade in 2011 with my daughter Isabel.

WABC studios in NYC filling in for Sean Hannity on radio.

Doing the media rounds at the 2012 Republican National Conventional in Tampa, FL.

Campaigning
for Congress in
Maryland in 2014.

Campaigning for Congress with my dedicated team of volunteers with loud yellow shirts.

Not a failure. A random picture kissing Paula.

With my daughter Amelia in our Severna Park, MD house.

Ringing the bell after my last cancer treatment at MD Anderson Cancer Center in Houston, TX.

At the White House South Grounds when Donald J. Trump accepted the Republican nomination for President in 2020.

Guest hosting *Fox & Friends* with Ainsley Earhardt and Steve Doocy.

Paula and me at the floor of the Nasdaq minutes after Rumble went public.

In NYC on the set of my show *Unfiltered* with Paula and Amelia.

Dinner with President Trump in New Jersey.

physical with any of these lunatics, no doubt it could have been a career ender. Or worse. I probably would have wound up in jail given what I was thinking of doing. But there was a bigger gift. For the first time, I saw firsthand, from the victim's perspective, what we were fighting for. Again, it's one thing to watch a riot on television. You may know what it is and what it looks like, but you have no true concept of what the reality is until you are on the ground in the middle of it. At that moment, experiencing the unhinged, uneducated, uncivilized rage of people who simply wanted to destroy human lives as well as what our country stands for, I had a much better understanding of what we are up against as conservatives. And it reminded me, if I'm ever in a position of political power, that any idiot can protect his political friends' right to speak. It's what you do when your political opponents want to speak that's the real marker of courage.

The DC mayor showed no courage on this night.

None of this happened by accident. These people were on the streets, terrorizing, burning, looting, and worse because they knew they could get away with it. There were no consequences. It was the result of failed liberal policies, and we saw it over and over and over that summer across other cities in America that had become victimized by these same weak, failed policies. None of this was an accident.

Today, whenever I need a reminder of why we need to fight back against woke culture and the destructive left-wing agenda that enables and fuels this kind of mayhem, I think back to August 2020 and the gift of clarity I received that night.

12

*"Success is not final, failure is not fatal:
it is the courage to continue that counts."*

—COMMONLY ATTRIBUTED
TO WINSTON S. CHURCHILL

There I was, sitting in my basement with a bunch of moving blankets and $10,000 of equipment that I had no idea how to use. All that stuff Paula charged to a credit card because we were running out of money, and I knew nothing from nothing about podcasting. But for me, expressing myself had become like a drug. I was doing so much public speaking that I felt like I had something to offer this new podcast medium. I was taking a chance on podcasting as well because it wasn't nearly as popular as it is now. But I figured it was worth the risk.

I didn't even know how to upload a podcast to Apple, or any platform for that matter. Thankfully, Paula was tech savvy, and so a lot of this fell on her. She told me, "I can figure out a lot, but I'm not ready to become an audio engineer. What the heck, I'm not MacGyver." And it was like that. Everything had to be jury-rigged and put together basically with spit and bubblegum (and those moving company blankets).

I remembered when I was running for Senate, I used to do a lot of radio interviews at WCBM in Baltimore, a legacy talk radio station. I always enjoyed talking to the *Morning Show* producer, Joe Armacost. He had always liked me, liked what I had to say, and seemed to get where I was coming from. Joe's a hard-nosed, middle-class working guy who reminded me a lot of the people from my neighborhood.

Joe is also a musician who had worked in radio for decades, so he knew what he was talking about. He saw something in me in this content production space that maybe I didn't see in myself. He sensed something, so I called him up. I said, "Joe, do you think you could help us out and help us get a podcast together? I don't have any money. I can't pay you for now, but if something happens with this, I promise I will take care of you." Joe said he would help me out despite unknown upsides, based solely on faith. That's why I am, to this day, ferociously loyal to him. He helped me get everything off the ground.

The launch of the podcast was me kind of acting out of desperation in a way, reacting to two failures. First, a failure to win the congressional race. Second, I was really interested in a radio job, but I was only getting lip service and not a hard offer from anyone. The attitude was that there's not a lot of real estate on the radio, and we're not tearing down a house for you. I was just too green and too new.

So, I started the podcast and took the lead.

When I listen to those first episodes in 2015 (you can probably find them on SoundCloud), I can tell I'm completely making it up as I go along. I had no idea how to put a show together or how to format it, because I had never done this before. I handled the episodes like I would handle a speech. I would just riff on things that mattered to me, get some thoughts together, and see where it went. When we first put it on SoundCloud, we didn't have any idea about music clearances and permissions. Talk about an epic fail. Without any copyright clearance, it got ripped down immediately. Another reason I needed Joe's help.

When I listen today, it is clear I did not know what I was doing. But it was oddly entertaining, like *Dan Bongino's Stream of Consciousness*. It was me and Joe in this tiny closet in my basement, with blankets on the wall to handle the sound issues. Forget about a professional studio, this was like an underground bunker. Everything was rigged from junk. It's like when I was a kid, and we couldn't afford Cheerios, so we got the no-frills brand of cereal. This was the equivalent of that no-frills cereal.

We bought furniture that was so cheap it would break when you'd attempt to drill a hole in it. The studio consisted of moving blankets, duct tape, a couple of rusted screws, and the equipment Paula bought with the credit card.

Then the strangest thing happened. People started responding to the show. The potential audience back then was a sliver of what it is now. But somehow, as limited as that was, we did well. In just a few weeks, we had made the top of the charts in terms of conservative talk podcasts. In that subcategory, we were doing very well. We were overwhelmed, but it was not happening by accident. I had nothing to lose, and I was always an activist first, so I spoke about these topics not as a talk show host but as an activist. We were hungry. It's like when cinematic fighter Clubber Lang was training in the dingy garage, and Rocky was out there kissing girls and signing autographs. We were the hungry ones. We were Clubber. I had gone back to square one, driven back there by failures. These are great moments because they teach you how to fight harder, not because of some inherent moral qualifications you have, but because of a survival instinct to stay alive.

Joe had been doing talk radio for so long, so he added some great structure to the show. I didn't always agree with him, but I trusted him. He would never change the content, just the structure (that's the way it still is today after eight years of working together). We started picking up serious steam. And as we did, and the show downloads started to pile up, some radio people started to take notice. I was getting lots of invites to be a regular guest on many shows. I was on lots of national shows, also doing fill-in work for Sean Hannity and Mark Levin. But the highlight was when Rush Limbaugh mentioned me on his radio show. Rush was the godfather (more on that soon). A mention by Rush Limbaugh was like being anointed. Now I felt like I belonged.

As things started to continue to pick up, I kept thinking to myself, I've got to make a choice. I had this conversation in my head. I said to myself, this is the most dangerous moment. Now you have something to lose. I had built an audience, sponsors were getting ready to come in, national syndicators were contacting me, and places wanted to partner with the podcast, but now I had to ask myself, am I ready to go for it?

All I could think about was Howard Stern in the movie about his life, *Private Parts* (based on his bestselling book). I had grown up listening to Howard, which makes his current tilt toward liberal politics all the more troubling for me. He meant something to me growing up.

He had been part of my morning routine. There's a moment in the movie where he's talking to his first wife Alison. He looks at her and says, "I have to be myself on the radio and tell the truth. I have to go all the way." I said the same thing to Paula. Just like the movie scene. She wasn't as approving as Howard's wife. It was more like, "Go all the way…but don't really go all the way… be careful." I decided I was going to say, "Screw the rules. There are one million talk radio rules. Many of the rules are bullshit. You stop thinking about the content when you start obeying all the rules."

I was going to let it all hang out and do the show I wanted. I figured by doing what was in my heart, I could never run for office again. I'd be burning too many bridges. Politics was over for me (or so I thought). Financially, we still had no real money. I was making some money guest hosting, but nothing was happening financially yet with the podcast.

I was about $50,000 in debt. But I sensed change happening. Again, my experience in politics taught me about what they call the "Big Mo." The concept of momentum. And it was real. You can't explain it. You just feel it. And so then we made a big move.

Paula's mom lived in Florida. I knew Paula wanted to be closer to her. My brother had left Maryland to go back to New York and there wasn't a lot keeping us there. So we moved to Palm City, Florida, close to my mother-in-law, and I did the podcast remotely with Joe. It was what my family needed. My youngest was too young to know the difference. But Isabel, who was about eleven at the time, definitely missed her friends, so it was tough for her. But we settled in. I got used to the power of the sun. It just does something for you. The power of the sun is real. If this seems like a melodramatic non sequitur maybe it is, but nonetheless, that Florida sun is life changing. (My pitch for conservatives to move to Florida is now over.)

Feeding off that new energy, the shows got better. We were doubling our audience every few months. Ten thousand, thirty thousand, fifty thousand, one hundred thousand—really exploding. The move to Florida was good for me.

There's a magic marker in podcasts where people finally decide they will invest in you. Once you get to about thirty thousand downloads, people in the business start wanting to look at your show. And we hit that fast. I got a call from a woman named Kelli who worked with Westwood One, one of the largest syndicators of radio programs, and they were venturing into the podcast space. She expressed an interest in the podcast. I didn't know Kelli's politics, nor did I care—she just had a knack for finding talent. She said, "I think your show is going to be something special. We want to talk to you." The show kept growing faster and faster and then some money started to come in from sponsors. Even though I said I was ready to "go all the way," now I had something to lose. Look, money is corrupting. Anyone who tells you they are above that is full of it. When money starts coming in, especially when you were a kid who grew up eating bologna sandwiches for dinner, and now you're making in one week what you made for a year as a Secret Service agent, well, some hard choices will soon follow.

Within a year or so in Florida, all of our financial problems were over. No matter how much money came in, I swore to myself I would never change the show. I told Westwood One and anybody else interested in a partnership, I will be doing *my* show. Nothing was going to change. I never wanted to be held hostage by a bank account.

With the kind of success we started enjoying, of course, the militant left tried to shut us down by going after our sponsors.

They are a one-trick pony. This is all they've got. Just know, when I got threats of a boycott by liberal groups, I'd simply be on the back of my deck smoking a cigar. I could not give a fuck. (Yes, I fully understand that expletives are a sometimes-artificial means of eliciting emotion done at the expense of your own morality. But I think you'll understand that this is one of the few times in the book that the word "fuck" is perfectly appropriate.) This bunch of mini-communist fascists trying to shut down free expression would not and will not ever stop me. We treated our sponsors like gold, and so I wasn't too concerned about the threats we started receiving. The fact that we were being targeted meant we were flying over the right targets. If a company paid for a sixty-second ad, I would give them two minutes. We spoiled our sponsors, and we still do. We didn't take holidays off. We over-delivered to our sponsors. Sponsors were raking it in, and we had people fighting to be part of our show.

We had the number two conservative podcast after years of hard work, right behind Ben Shapiro, and our growth was organic. Our marketing budget was basically zero. As a matter of fact, our operational budget was nothing to write home to your mother about either. Paula was the producer. We didn't want to get in over our heads, so we ran lean and mean. I loved having Paula produce the shows. It was fun. In the beginning we figured living together and then working together on the show was going to be a disaster. But I think even she would attest to the fact that outside of a few minor disagreements we had, it really was a simple process because there's no better judge of me than her. A lot of that early growth was simply due to Paula giving me a thumbs up or thumbs down on what I was doing. Not to mention, she was the manager, administrator, file editor, producer, accountant; she was everything. Life was good. Right before the 2020 election, we were number one in our category. We had the fastest-growing conservative website and an enormous social media presence. In short, we were killing it.

One day Paula said, "Something's going to go wrong." Huh? It was just a hunch she had, perhaps borne of failures finding us in the past. And she was right. Don't ask me how. She just had a feeling. Something was just going to go wrong. It's hard to explain how real the feeling was. Like the "Big Mo," the "Big Slow Mo" is also very real.

And then January 6 happened.

The so-called insurrection (give me a break). Regardless of the misreporting, it was a disaster on every level for us. The election was a mess and both Georgia Senate races went down in flames for our side. After January 6, the podcast audience suffered. We lost a lot of listeners. The hurt from that was that we had been growing for five years straight at that point. Forget about shrinking. We had always been growing. Shrinking for us was not growing, so that's why this was exceptionally painful. We still had a good audience, but there were plenty of trouble signs now. It was enough to remind us not to take anything for granted. Even so, in those rough first months of 2021, I never gave up. A few sponsors bailed out. We never knew if it was financial or due to January 6. Regardless, I still did the podcast and put in my best effort. Maybe people needed a break from politics and that was it. I understood it. It was a tough time. But I kept plugging away because I felt I owed that to the audience. So I stuck to what I knew, passionately defending conservatism at any and all costs. Months went by, the audience started to filter back in, and it was rewarding to know that they might have lost a few battles but they still had their eyes on the prize in this big ideological cosmic war. The audience wasn't ready to give up. Nor was I.

Then the bottom really fell out. The conservative movement lost Rush Limbaugh. February 17, 2021. Talk about a dark day. I grew up on Rush. Hell, everybody grew up on Rush in the conservative movement. Rush *was* the conservative movement.

Rush was not just the MVP of talk radio. I think Mickey Mantle was the best center fielder of all time, which people can debate. But nobody argues about Rush Limbaugh. And Mickey Mantle did not invent the game of baseball. Rush Limbaugh essentially invented conservative talk radio. There had never been anything like him, and I don't think there ever will be. I grew up on him. He had gotten me through tough times. Sadly, I never got to know him. A relative of his worked with some of the Fox News hosts. I ran into her in the green room one day, and I told her that if I met him, it might not resonate much with him (not because of any character flaw in him but just because he's been told that by so many for more than thirty years), but it mattered to me. I wanted to be on the record in Rush's face. Weird or not, I just wanted him to know firsthand what I thought and felt about him. It is ironic, because now when people come up to me and pay a nice compliment, I'm always sure to look them in the eye and ask them their name, so I can let them know it mattered and that I appreciate what they are saying. But then he got sick, and I didn't want to make it about me.

I was in the shower one day, listening to him on the radio, not even knowing that would be his last show. If I had known, I would have gotten out of the shower, dried off, and sat there listening with rapt attention. It's as if you're listening to The Beatles' first album knowing it will be the last time it is played on planet earth.

You are going to listen to it differently when you know it's the last time. And I didn't do that. Nobody knew it was his last show, and it's not the same listening to a recording of that show today. You had to listen to it as it was happening. It's like watching Mariano Rivera come out of the Yankees bullpen that one last time. Yes, the replay will give you goose bumps. But nothing can match watching it in real time.

Then he was gone.

I had no established relationship with Westwood One at this point when it came to radio, just the podcast, and Rush Limbaugh was on a number of the big legacy Westwood One radio stations throughout the country.

Nobody knew what to do with the loss of Rush. I got a call, and they asked if I wanted that job. I couldn't believe it. I'd gone full circle. I didn't want it. It was an honor to be asked, but I really didn't want it. I loved the late, great New York Yankees Bobby Murcer (who replaced the Mick), but Bobby Murcer was no Mickey Mantle. Bobby would have told you that too. I didn't want to be Bobby Murcer. Nobody can replace the Mick. And I sure as shit was no Rush Limbaugh. But I thought more about it. About "going all the way." About being a "doer" and not just a talker. (Ironic, isn't it?) I had a moment with Paula, and I told her, even though I would never be Rush Limbaugh, at least I could be the best Dan Bongino I could be. And I would take that shot with the two rules that drive my career: I wasn't going to do it for money, and I was going to keep doing my show the way I did it. If you liked it, great, and if you didn't, there wasn't much I could do about it. The thing about replacing a legend is that you are never going to be that guy, so you better be *your* guy.

I decided that I would accept the offer.

Within a few months, everything would be tested when it came down to a fight over the vaccine. Cumulus Media, which was the parent company of Westwood One, established a vaccine mandate within the company, and it was a mandate that had teeth. It wasn't a mild suggestion. Obviously, this wasn't going to fly with me or my audience, and I did the best I could both on the air and behind the scenes to pressure them into changing it. It took a lot of energy out of my life and it put a lot of stress on my marriage but ultimately in the end, a contract is a contract. And there were other people involved, which meant their jobs were at stake too. It put me in a very challenging predicament, and this is one of those times where you have to make moral compromises that other people don't. All of a sudden, I was responsible for the jobs of a lot of people who helped to support the show. It's easy at that point to throw people under the bus and say, "This is bullshit. You all should have walked out," and I understand that. I do. But what about all of those jobs? What about the jobs of the people that left other jobs to come work for me? What do you do about them? So again, I had to make a moral compromise that I'm still not happy about. I'm not bragging about it. I'm just telling you. These are just the kind of things, when you have a show of that magnitude, where the considerations become different. All of a sudden, there is a lot of gray. Not everything is black-and-white. But what was black-and-white to me was that I wasn't going to accept that, and I was going to put Cumulus on notice publicly, stating that our relationship was over when this contract was done. A lot of people warned me not to do that. They said it would hurt the potential growth of the show. I disagreed. What radio stations want is someone who is going to stick to their guns. So I publicly stated on the air, at the end of that contract term, that

I was not going to be working for this company anymore. By the time this book is published, and you are reading it, I will still be on the air. Beyond that, I'm not sure what the future brings, but that was not a failure. I was not kidding when I said that.

13

*"Many of life's failures are people
who did not realize how close they were
to success when they gave up."*

—THOMAS A. EDISON

Making the transition to television, for me anyway, was never nerve racking or anxiety producing. When you talk to many people who are on television or the radio today, they will usually describe how awkward and uncomfortable it is in the beginning because of the nerves that can take over. It's a strange feeling to all of a sudden have a microphone in front of you or a camera alongside you. I think because I had already lived in several fairly high-profile universes, I was equipped for the transition. Within the Secret Service, I had been part of many high-level security meetings, and through jujitsu and the NYPD, I had developed a serious mental toughness. I was also quite good at detecting bullshit that, as I've learned, can really come in handy when you go in front of the cameras. Contrary to ever being nervous before radio or podcasting or television, I fed off the energy right from the get-go. It was exciting for me, even euphoric at times. Also, when I first started doing media "hits" as a wannabe politician, I was already a deep consumer of TV news. ("Hits" is one of those industry jargon terms that makes you sound cool when you say it. It simply means "appearance.") That made it even more exciting for me because all of a sudden, I was now walking onto the same sets and into the same studios that produced the news that I would listen to and watch every single day. It was surreal to be part of those worlds.

If you were to go back and look at my first appearance with Neil Cavuto on Fox News, it's easy to see that I'm not remotely nervous. It worked. It just felt natural to me. I became entranced with the idea that I could sit there and share my views about certain subjects and automatically connect with an audience. I think I was a quick study. One thing I learned right out of the gate by watching other guests was that if you got nervous, the audience would be able to smell it, and then they would get nervous for you. That creates a very uncomfortable experience for both the host and the audience. I knew that as a viewer at home. When I saw a guest get that deer-in-the-headlights look, it made me uncomfortable. It was like watching a failure in real time. I felt bad for them. Similarly, when I could tell that a guest was comfortable in the conversation, then I relaxed as a viewer and flowed with whatever was happening. I would pay closer attention. I would think about those things whenever I went on TV or the radio. The more comfortable I am, the more comfortable the audience will be. It was that simple for me.

Once I started getting regular bookings, I never wanted to stop. When I was running for office, I did anything I needed to do to get on television. It wasn't just that I enjoyed it. I also appreciated the fact that it helped build my profile and reach potential voters. There's a reason they call it "earned media." You have to earn the opportunity to speak for free in front of millions of people (and avoid having to pay for a TV commercial). There were days during campaigns when I would spend eight hours or more in a car to drive all the way up to Fox News in New York, do a series of shows, and then drive home the same day. I would leave sometimes at two o'clock in the morning to get there in time for a morning hit. Looking back on it, I almost can't believe the time and energy that I put into never missing a TV shot (and I also can't believe I never got in a car wreck driving back and forth).

After I ran for office and lost, as far as TV and radio went, the hits must have been going well because I kept getting invited back. Apparently, I was comfortable with the audience, and they were relatively comfortable with me. Not that I was any kind of viral sensation, but people seemed to enjoy what I had to say. The only problem was, in the years following my runs for office, I was now primarily getting boxed in as the "former Secret Service guy." Listen, I love defending the police and talking about the law; I always have, and I always will. But I had a lot of other interests as well that I felt as strong or stronger about. I had spent a number of years becoming friendly with producers who would call me back time and again, and they knew what I was capable of. It was not their fault. It's what producers do. They want subject matter experts. But as a result of my Secret Service expertise, I was getting pigeonholed. In a strange way, building my TV resume was becoming a failure because it was tough to break out of the law enforcement–talking head mold and the preconceived notion about who I was. I also wanted to be talking about tax policy, advocating for the Second Amendment, advocating for pro-life issues, and so forth. That's who I was. That's why I ran for office, and that's what I wanted to get across on television.

I wasn't getting paid in these early days, and money wasn't my primary objective. But I had a long-term goal that seemed like a far-off dream at the time: to become a Fox News contributor and to get paid for doing what I loved. I was doing my best to be a good team player and be there when they needed me. But again, I was ready to grow in my role. So I rolled the dice, and I took a chance.

The folks at Fox News—great people who I had very solid working relationships with, by the way—brought me up to New York after developing a small library of my hits. It was a meeting with the producers (along with people who booked all of the shows). It meant a lot to me that they cared enough to do this. It was a big roundtable meeting where the staff asked me questions about myself and how I saw myself on the network. It was in that meeting that I decided to take a chance and let them know that I needed to branch out from my role as a law enforcement expert. I say "chance" because this could have been cable news suicide. I would be suggesting to them that the area where I had the largest library of personal experience wasn't the one that I cared about the most. It's an odd stance to take. I could tell by the looks on some of the faces in the room that this was not what they expected. I think they were expecting me to continue to advocate for bookings as a law enforcement expert and talk about where we would take that. But I wanted more. And by asking for more, I knew I was taking a chance that they might move on from me and start booking someone else for these Secret Service/law enforcement stories.

Things got quiet for about a month after that meeting, and I thought, what have I done? This is a huge failure. I should have kept my mouth shut and done what I had been doing up to that point: stick to the law enforcement stories. But then, one by one, I started getting calls to come on and discuss other issues. Everyone in the room, without really letting on in front of me, understood that I was becoming a passionate conservative who could talk about everything from inflation to economics to the presidency and beyond. So thankfully everything worked out, and I became a regular contributor on the network. What looked like a potentially catastrophic failure had turned in my favor.

But there's another event, or rather series of events, at Fox News that I think many may describe as a failure for me. At one point I think I would have as well, but now I'm not so sure.

One night I was booked on Sean Hannity's TV show, and I wound up debating veteran newsman Geraldo Rivera. It wasn't meant to be some fiery debate segment. I didn't know him at all. Zero. We had just wound up on the segment together. We got into a blowout yelling match that I believe involved police issues and immigration issues. It went nuclear. In television, you can get minute-by-minute breakdowns on the ebb and flow of the audience ratings within each segment, and that particular segment grew by the second. After that, whenever Geraldo and I were both together, the same thing seemed to evolve. We would fight about almost anything. People would ask me afterward if it was real. Of course, it was real. Fox News is not the WWE. I would get asked a lot if we "liked" each other. That's a relative term. I'm in the business of defending conservatism. That's my job. Geraldo is in the business of defending whatever Geraldo wants to defend. He earned that right. But I take no prisoners on TV, and I don't let personal relationships get in the way of anything. Neither did Geraldo. That's probably why the segments got so spicy! Geraldo has always been nice to me in person, and I think it's genuine. We've never hung out or socialized. I think I've been polite right back to him. It's not about that. In the heat of live debating in front of millions of people, you have to defend your position and sometimes, to quote rapper Nelly, it was just getting "hot in herre."

One of the golden rules of television is that what happens on the air stays on the air. And that's how I am with Geraldo. No matter how heated things have gotten, whenever we've seen each other, we don't dwell on our grievances. That wouldn't be professional. It's a "hey man, how's the family?" kind of thing. And then back on the air to fight again.

After a number of these highly charged segments, I began to worry that I was failing in the eyes of the audience because it may have seemed like I was losing my cool. You can't go on and just scream every night. You have to understand where the lines are. And they are fine lines. When I passionately debate with Geraldo, which some might see as arguing, I am representing my true beliefs. The one thing I have to keep in mind is to never lose the crux of the argument (something I'm still working on). Again, you can't just yell to yell. There has to be substance, even at a higher volume.

Something else I've noticed during my years on television: there are people who, anticipating a harsh debate with you on the air, will try and make friends in the green room to potentially defuse any upcoming tension. I don't go for that. It happened to me once on a television show in Virginia. There was going to be a debate over Second Amendment rights, and the guy I would be debating tried to become my friend in the green room. I just said hello and kept my head down. Again, I wasn't going to be impolite, but I didn't want to chat. I knew for a fact this was a guy who was trying to take my guns away. And yours. That pissed me off, and I wasn't going to act like it didn't. I didn't engage beyond a terse hello. And then I went out and destroyed him in that on-air debate.

Take care of your business on the air.

I respect Geraldo. We are both arthritic, collapsing, and falling apart, yet we enjoy sparring with each other. The only failure from those debates, again, is that I sometimes lose focus of the argument. That can happen in the heat of battle. It's happened to me a couple of times. I've regretted it, but I've also learned from it.

14

*"I haven't failed. I've just found ten thousand
ways that don't work."*

—THOMAS A. EDISON

One of the things I had naïvely neglected in the early days of my success as a content producer of podcasts and radio and television commentaries was the drive on the left to censor any ideas they found uncomfortable. I can't emphasize enough the importance of this issue in my life. It's literally the genesis that drives my life energy. I'm not being hyperbolic. Outside of my God, my kids, and my wife, this is it. Since you're reading this book right now, I need you to really stop, focus, and pay attention to what I'm about to tell you. I need you to understand as a listener, a friend, or someone who just casually picked up this book, that the story I'm about to tell you—about fighting censorship-loving, totalitarian leftists—is the driving force of my life. I said once on a show I hosted, "I live my life to own the libs." What we are fighting are not just random, off-the-shelf bad guys. It is genuine, generational evil. This is the real fight. When I go to the pearly gates of heaven and I have to present my resume to the Almighty about the bad stuff I fought against, these are the people who are going to be the first line. They are that bad.

Initially, I failed to comprehend just how destructive and malevolent they are. It's ironic that they tweet about fascism all the time, claiming that they are warriors against it, when in reality they emulate the tactics of these generationally destructive fascists and totalitarians themselves. And I failed to comprehend that in the beginning.

I failed and made a big mistake by misjudging their intentions. At the time, I assumed that pointing out their hypocrisy, challenging their "hatred" of fascism even though they emulated fascism, might make them realize how foolish and misguided they looked. Another fail. I learned fast: hypocrisy doesn't matter to them. It is all about hierarchy. That's what totalitarians crave. Power. They were in charge, and they wanted you to know that they had the power and they wanted to abuse it.

Power is the coin of the realm with this bunch. When the socialists in Cuba—the Che Guevara crowd—put people up against the wall and shot them, they didn't care that he was being called a hypocrite by the parents of those people being killed in cold blood. They'll take that.

Unquestionably, this underestimation was my failure. However, it led to greater success, and I wouldn't change anything. (Remember the theme of this book, folks.)

They may (and I say "may" because nobody ever said to us they were leaving because of these fascistic pressure groups—I'm guessing, but I'll put a point on the board for them) have succeeded early on in picking off a few random sponsors here and there (these totalitarian leftists were obsessed with trying to censor my show), but they didn't realize that they incentivized me to become a tech entrepreneur and a major cog in this new freedom of speech movement. I traded some short-term stress dealing with a random sponsor once in a blue moon, but this all led to a long-term sense of security from the free-speech parallel economy that I and others were busy creating.

My underestimation of their totalitarian impulse was the key to my future success. The battles suck while they are going on. As most do. You think to yourself, can I just have a peaceful week? But that's not what sharpens steel. You need the confrontation, and I got it.

I started to ask myself real questions like, Do I want to spend the rest of my life battling with a bunch of two thousand–followers, junk food–addicted losers in their basement threatening my sponsors? Or would I rather work with companies that don't give a shit about politics, believe in themselves, and just want to grow their brands? That's an easy answer.

I started to figure out the left's game plan, and of course, most of them had articles. Ironically, these were old articles they had written where they had said grotesquely inappropriate things, revealing themselves as the same kind of bigots they were baselessly accusing people like me of being. I started fighting back, and every time they came at me, I would tweet back an article exposing their hypocrisy, tagging my sponsors with "are these the kinds of people *you* want to do business with?" I actually learned a lot from them about how to throw their tactics right back in their faces, and twice as hard.

Once you point out their frailties, all of a sudden they back down because they don't have the fight, gusto, or the desire to try and keep the beach ball of freedom underwater. That takes too much energy for these cowards. And there's not enough Ben & Jerry's ice cream in the world to feed these losers with the energy to fight against genuine street fighters.

I started to think to myself, wouldn't it be nice (and necessary) to help build a parallel economy where both conservative and liberal commentators could operate in a capitalistic, free-from-tyranny environment, and not have to worry about political censorship? "Just don't break the law, and you are free to express in here without censorship." That would be the most important rule of the road.

So, I started searching for companies that I could partner with. That's why I came to the Parler team. They were doing some ads on my show, buying some spots that were successful. I believed in them. Twitter was engaged in some heavy censorship of conservatives at that point. I had met some of the Parler people earlier on, I liked them, and felt it was time to take the partnership to the next level.

They had been up and running for maybe a year or so, and they had done okay, but they weren't a household name. We had some conversations about a business relationship, and I wound up taking an equity stake because there's no better way to put skin in the game—than to actually get skin in the game.

But it was kind of a failure in the beginning. See, I'm not a tech guy. Even though I invest in tech companies, I'm still not a tech guy. Peter Thiel and Elon Musk are tech guys. They understand the tech world, and so it was an early failure on my part to not better educate myself on the topic. You don't have to understand all of the inner tech workings, but you have to have people around you who can speak to you in a jargon-free way about what it is you are involved in. Remember the "flux capacitor" in *Back to the*

Future? It was the core component of Dr. Emmett Brown's DeLorean time machine. But nobody knew what it was. You have to know exactly what it is you are invested in. Again, I didn't get the tech side of it, a failure on my part. I should've done a better job of vetting the tech, but I was so passionate about what they were doing that I believed in the mission, and I became blinded by that.

I learned a few things in business school I've never forgotten. One of the concepts, "negation," came from a very smart business professor who said, "It's difficult to sell a product or service via negation—i.e., telling people what you are *not*."

I'm not going sell you a book by telling you what is not in it. When marketing, you sell a product based on the substance of the product. Same thing in politics. It isn't enough to bash the other guy. You have to talk about what *you* are going to do.

Given the hatred that conservatives had toward the censorship autonomy that was developing via Twitter, Facebook, YouTube, and other platforms, I sensed an opening that defied conventional logic. I said to some of the folks at Parler, "I think this is one of the first times in the history of marketing a product where we can sell this thing almost exclusively by what it isn't."

So many people enjoyed microblogging but hated the bullshit politics that were developing, so I also told Parler, "What if we just said hey, it's like Twitter without the bad shit? I'm reasonably sure we could take this thing through the roof." I understand that this is probably not going to make the opening chapter of any business textbook, but sometimes the best rules of operating a business are the simplest ones, and this seemed pretty simple to me.

"We are not Twitter." That was the pitch. There was so much hatred toward Twitter that it made sense. People required no explanation of what Twitter was. They knew. And conservatives hated it. I know there were some doubters, but there were some believers too. Enough believers at Parler who figured, "Hey this guy built a big podcast. He can't be that stupid." They agreed to let me give it a shot.

So that's what I did. I went on the show, and I told people that Parler was Twitter without the blatant censorship, and I made a passionate case for it. At first, it was like a gradual slow burn. And then it started to take hold...

I knew I could make this thing a success if I sold it passionately day after day. So I spent hours and hours on social media talking about it, responding to attacks on it from the left, and the app started to creep up. And then it started to grow geometrically. At one point, we woke up and we were the number one app in the world. Not in our category *but in the world*. I felt like this was it. This was an earth-shaking moment. We had taken on the big tech titans and reached the top of the mountain. The 2020 election was right around the corner, and we were the number one app in the world. That was an enormous accomplishment, especially given all we were up against.

I was just an equity holder. I wasn't privy to a lot of internal discussions, and not being a tech guy, it was tough for me to anticipate the bugs that began to happen. But the most remarkable thing was, even with the bugs, the app continued to grow, and we were number one multiple days at a time. We were very proud, Paula and me. As someone more familiar in the tech space (it was her job), she totally got it. But one of the best parts? Watching the liberals melt down. It illustrated that they have no dignity or principles. For years they told us that "Twitter is a free market! They can do what they want when it comes to censoring conservatives!

Twitter is a private company!" Conservatives said, "Fine, screw you, we're going to go build our own."

And we did.

Even with the bugs it was a hit. And the left lost their minds. "How dare you go off and become a big success!" It was the weirdest thing. If there was ever an episode of my life that in one moment helped me understand with clarity the entire totalitarian leftist regime, that was it. "You stay here; we will censor you and destroy you. You leave here, and we will follow you and still try and censor you and destroy you." It's pathological.

These words are not hyperbolic. These are facts, and I mean every single syllable. And then some. This is the left. When you see them up close and personal, getting in your face and trying to destroy you, you understand what they are all about. You realize who these people really are. All of a sudden, the history of fascism and totalitarianism makes complete sense. The left became obsessed with following us, and they wanted nothing more than to see this platform fail and for everyone involved with it to suffer. These people would physically hurt you if they could.

So I noticed this pattern where liberals would go set up fake accounts with Nazi symbols and other offensive and horrible things, and then they would begin trying to sabotage the platform from within. They would put a Parler post up with some deranged thing, which would then generate a unique news cycle within liberal circles. Self-fulfilling bullshit. I'm not saying every distasteful post was that, but there was a clear pattern there.

They were clearly trying to destroy it. And they weren't the only ones.

15

*"Failures have been errors in judgment,
not of intent."*

—GENERAL ULYSSES S. GRANT

After January 6 happened, the left sensed an opportunity to advance the totalitarian football down the field. And they were right. It was there for them. One thing they rarely seem to miss is a chance to exploit their oppressive, draconian agenda, and leveraging any kind of tragedy to their own advantage.

This was a huge political opening for them. No conservative I knew believed the United States would sanction violence against itself at any time. Everybody wished things had gone down differently. The left was fighting a conservative phantom. Something that simply did not exist.

And no matter what, Parler was going to be public enemy number one. It was the only social media space where some modicum of free speech flourished at the time. So of course, Parler took the blame. You can read the government's own charging documents and see that all kinds of social media platforms—Facebook,

THE GIFT OF FAILURE

Twitter, YouTube, and others—had similar issues the media hacks claimed were unique to Parler, but it didn't matter. It was all about Parler. We were the most convenient target because we were the only ones running against the cancel culture movement. The narrative was going to be, "Look what they did! Look what they did on Parler!" And the anti-Parler movement was created to destroy the only free-speech vehicle in a liberal-dominated social media space. Paula had said something bad was going to happen and that sense she had, whatever cosmic energy she felt, well, she was right on the money.

I knew the "Big Mo" had changed. I knew we were in trouble. I got a call from a guy I do business with who had been involved with Parler. He told me there was a backend administrative company that was going to cancel their Parler contract over the new phony January 6 "insurrection" outcries. Even though it wasn't a catastrophic or earth-shaking moment yet, as I paced outside in front of my house, walking around in the dark getting bitten by mosquitoes, I knew this was the beginning of the end. That's the thing with bloodthirsty cancel culture goons. When they smell the blood, biology takes over. There is no super ego. It's only id.

I knew it because I finally understood who the left truly was. They would legitimately hurt you if they could. Physically. And this was the next best thing. I mean that. (And this might be a failure because in writing classes they will tell you to never compose a sentence like "I mean that." But it's true. There's no other way to say it.)

If this one company had just sucked it up and said, "You know, this seems kind of ridiculous. It's a dark moment in our history. Let's let it play out, give it some time, and let it resolve," that would've been the end of it. And Parler likely would have survived intact. The left would've done what they always do when their diapers get full: move on to some other outrage. They are not warriors, they have no grit, and they prey on the weak.

We legitimately had done something special. The platform wasn't perfect. I had no role in the management of the company, so I really couldn't affect that. Watching it start to evaporate before my eyes, outside of a death in the family, was one of my lowest moments. I just couldn't believe what I was seeing. I couldn't believe this was America. It was sad on so many levels—not just the money but the principle. We had been *number one*. That a bunch of Ben & Jerry's eaters could sit in their basement and take down what could've been the most successful microblogging platform in the history of the United States with just a snap of their fingers…disappointment doesn't seem strong enough to describe what I felt in view of this failure, which never should have been a failure to begin with. I was mortified. Depressed. Disillusioned.

And pissed.

We had worked so hard. It was such a good idea. But the destructive capabilities of these people are their reason for being. Even talking about it now, I still get upset. It was the beginning of the end, but it wasn't the end yet. I thought maybe some of these companies would grow some balls and stand up. Allegations that could not even be proven, things that other companies were certainly guilty of, and *we* were the ones being targeted. Now it's fairly obvious that Google is a company run by left-wingers. Still, I had a small sense of hope that maybe, just maybe, this one time they would do the right thing versus doing the "easy" thing. Shame on me. Google pulled Parler from their app store. It's hard to run a business in a tech-heavy environment when that happens. I can't say I was surprised. But it was no less devastating.

We were being held to an artificial standard. The left craved power—that's what totalitarianism is. It's not a double standard. It's one standard: "Fuck you, *we* have the power." Apple will cater to anybody out there, but when it came to Parler, they were more than happy to dump us as well. That happened shortly after Google pulled the proverbial trigger. That one really hurt, because prior to Apple dropping us from the app store, they had done their best to challenge law enforcement on all kinds of what they referred to as "civil rights issues": hacking into bad guys' phones, and so on. So the bad guys were good enough to save, but the free-speech good guys weren't?

Once you lose Apple and Google, it's pretty much over. It was like watching a death in slow motion. It was like watching hair get pulled out strand by strand. Then Amazon pulled us down from Amazon Web Services, effectively dismantling the website. Now, with no app and no website, Parler was effectively killed at that point. We couldn't believe it. It was like living in North Korea. People with absolutely zero skin in the game, who'd never expended one ounce of sweat, many who have never had a job in their lives—these liberal activists, the ones who dress up in fake Antifa costumes—how do they get to determine who gets to operate on the internet and who doesn't? But this was the world we lived in. It wasn't like living in a constitutional republic anymore. Yes, we have a constitution that says we are free to speak. But are we? In name only perhaps. "You're free to speak...but not on any platforms you choose to speak on."

The Orwellian "Newspeak" in the so-called digital democracy was beyond oppressive. It was horrifying. In the libertarian and conservative view of digital democracy, it means allowing people to speak and argue out their ideas on public forums. That's not what the left thinks. We lived by it. We never censored liberals. Parler even put a "reward" out for liberals to come on over to Parler—that's how badly we wanted both sides represented.

So, we were all but done. After Amazon, I started thinking, this is truly catastrophic. In the blink of an eye, we went from building something that was going to change the world to having essentially nothing.

These big tech companies are all run by the same Silicon Valley leftists. They collude with the government to crush their competitors, yet the left claims they are against monopolies. It's all bullshit. Frauds. They'll kiss the ass of a monopoly in a heartbeat to advance their political agenda.

Now, this is the point where any leftist reading this book (and I give you credit if you are) will take a victory lap. Go for it. Enjoy it. Savor it. Because this is also the part where I tell you to shove it up your ass, and I stick it back to you. Enjoy the moment of triumph. I assure it will be short-lived. Grab another pint of Cherry Garcia. I'll wait.

A normal person would say, "You can't beat these guys. Have a nice day." Not me. Out of the depths of my despair, I was ready to fight back. This time I was straight-up pissed. Furious. I didn't need any time to reflect as I did with medical school. I was simply ready to fight. After watching them take down Parler, I was now going to dedicate the rest of my life to evening up the score. I'd love to tell you that my foray into additional tech investments after this was due to some Elon Musk–like entrepreneurial endeavor to send a man to space. But that would be a failure because that would be bullshit. It was just straight-up rage. I saw what they did, and I wanted a reckoning. And if that reckoning resulted in the expansion of civil liberties and free speech, then all the merrier.

After all, rage can be a positive thing, as long as you don't use it for the wrong reason. And there's no better reason than defending and advocating for free speech for everyone—even your loudest political opponent.

And that's what led to Rumble.

16

*"I don't fear failure. I only fear the slowing up
of the engine inside of me which is saying,
'Keep going, someone must be on top, why not you?'"*

—GENERAL GEORGE S. PATTON JR.

I'm not sure this is the greatest story to fit in a book about failures but regardless...it's one I feel I must tell. When your body fails you, no thanks to you, it forces you to learn important lessons, whether you want to or not.

I had become kind of cocky about my health. I worked out religiously, barely drank, never smoked, and never did drugs (at least not the nonprescription kind with the funny names). Weren't we all told growing up that those were the keys to a healthy lifestyle, A to Z? And I wasn't missing a letter. When you do all of that and there's no history of serious disease in your family, you never consider that anything bad is going to creep up on you one day.

Like my Senate race, a sane person would've looked at the probabilities and said, "Are you crazy?" But to get into a race like that, or to get through medical school, I had to tell myself that this had a small possibility of success. But in my head I thought, this is very real, and I'm going to defy the odds.

But it's the opposite when it came to my health.

It's one thing to be a one-in-ten-thousand shot when you run for office, but when it comes to your health and something bad happens, you think—this can't be me. But it does go both ways. Lightning can strike in either direction, and sometimes it can really hurt. Especially a direct hit.

I never considered I would be one of those people who would get sick. Maybe it was naïveté or maybe it was just present-day confirmation bias.

In other words, you're not sick, so therefore you're never going to get sick. But it had never occurred to me, so there was no plan if something happened to me. It probably would've been great to develop a detailed backup plan. But that was a failure on my part.

Life was going great. I was having a grand old time. Even though the Parler thing didn't work out as planned, I still felt like I was accomplishing big things.

Outside of some minor arthritis issues (after an attempt at boxing, which helped me develop a face for radio), I was generally in good shape. I loved jujitsu, and all of the stereotypes you've heard about people who do Brazilian jujitsu are true. The joke is: "How do you know someone does Brazilian jujitsu? Don't worry, they'll tell you." And even though I would never get into a bar fight willingly at this stage of my life, I took jujitsu and boxing because I never wanted to negotiate again from a point of weakness in my life. Growing up in New York City (I don't want to exagger-ate, it wasn't *Straight Outta Compton*), street fighting was a pretty common thing. As I wrote earlier, the first time I got into a really bad street fight, it changed me. And I found myself negotiating my way in or out of fights based on what the outcome would be. That was something, of course, I didn't want to do anymore, which is what propelled me into boxing and jujitsu. But back to our story. I was in my midforties. I would come home every Saturday from jujitsu class all beaten up, barely able to move as the "sore chemicals" started to kick in, and the weekend would become simply an adventure in recovery (and lots of Advil). Paula would say with a joking smile, "Hey, time to wrap this up. What are you training for? You're forty-five years old. Your shot at the UFC is long past." In addition to wanting to look after my family and not negotiate from a point of weakness, I just loved the spirit of competition, and I loved being able to roll with these young kids and show them that a guy old enough to be their father could still hack it.

But eventually, the kids start getting the better of you, and biology takes over. There's only one Tom Brady.

And I ain't it.

I'd been rolling around with this kid named Lucas at a Brazilian jujitsu school run by a talented guy named Joe in Jupiter, Florida. This kid was way too fast for me. The first thing that goes with age is raw speed. And even though he was a belt below me, the joke in jujitsu is that every ten years, you lose a belt level. So technically, we were even, although that's probably just an excuse for my failure. Reflexes go quickly. I just wasn't quick enough. The kid came around, accidentally kneed me in the face, and gave me the most vicious black eye I think I've ever had (and I've had a few). Needless to say, the Fox News team wasn't too crazy about that. I didn't have a show yet, but I was doing regular appearances and this was not a good look. After all, it's Fox News, not Foxy Boxing. And the last thing I am is foxy.

It's one thing to be eighteen years old with a black eye. It's another thing to be forty-five with a lot of makeup on trying to hide it. I decided it was time to start doing my jujitsu training at home.

So, I started taking private lessons from a couple of different guys, Steve and Harlan. One day, Harlan choked me out badly. It was like in the cartoons when you get banged in the head and the stars circle around. I was *out*. It wasn't excessively violent; it was just a pretty good episode of oxygen deprivation. I was getting ready to go on Fox on Monday morning and while shaving, when I turned my face to the right, to shave the left side of my face, I noticed a prominent lump on my neck. A normal person would say, "This sucks. I should go to a doctor." But not me. Again, this is a book about failures. I just figured it was a fatty tumor. No big deal. Maybe it was related to getting choked. The idea of a cancerous tumor never entered my mind.

I don't like going to doctors. Ironic, because I wanted to be one a long time ago, and while I really respect the field, I just hate going to a doctor's office (I prefer the dentist).

Luckily, I had a friend who was a local head and neck surgeon. I called him, and I said, "Steve, I have to come in. I have a lump on my neck, probably a fatty tumor..." He said, "Sure." So I went by the office, and I could tell right away he was concerned. This was during the early days of COVID, so everything was shut down, but he arranged for me to go to a local Cleveland Clinic facility. Luckily, he knew the radiation oncologist—really nice guy—and he agreed to sit there during the MRI. That was great because then I wouldn't have to wait for it to be read. They laid me down in the machine, put a cage over my face (which freaked me out because I'm claustrophobic), and gave me some headphones to play music (that machine is *loud*).

I was in the machine for about twenty minutes or so, and I couldn't move my head, but I moved my eyes over to see the radiologist. At this point, I had no worries at all. They tell you in the headphones, "Okay, we are wrapping up." Then they roll you slowly out of the machine, which makes it more dramatic because you see this guy standing there over you, and you can't move your head. Todd, his name was, was staring down at me somberly but not appearing overly concerned. But it's enough that I'm concerned that he is somber and not overly concerned. I said to him, "It's a fatty tumor…right?" He said, "I think we need to put on your clothes and then we need to talk."

Oh shit.

He brought me back to a little room, showed me the images from the MRI, and said, "I can't tell you what it is. But I can tell you what it isn't, and it's no fatty tumor. Fat would be white." What I had on my neck was big, and it was jet black.

They say time slows down in moments like this. I remember in graduate school, doing some homework and learning that there are actual bio-chemical reasons that cause the sensation of time speeding up or slowing down. How we comprehend time is a byproduct of biological processes that speed up and slow down based on stress. Maximum stress equals maximum time elongation. So this time, the moment seemed to last forever. To comprehend what I was hearing, I was slowing things down.

I walked outside of the facility in shock, and that eighth of a mile or so walk to my car was the longest distance I have ever felt. I didn't know what to do, so I started to call Paula, while at the same time thinking that maybe I should do this in person. But I needed to talk at that moment. It was like an information bomb that was going to explode out of me. I just had to get rid of it. So I called Paula from the car. "We need to talk. And it isn't good. It's a tumor." She couldn't believe it either.

It seemed so unfair, as if there is fairness in the world. I say that all the time on the radio, and I truly mean it. There are circumstances in this life, and there are responses to them. There's no fairness.

I came home, Paula was outside with the dog, and she was crying. The dog had strolled over as she always does to the neighbor's yard. We hugged in the neighbor's front yard and Paula said, "What are we going to do?" I said, "I have no idea." I had no backup plan. As I said earlier, I had never anticipated this, and so we started to process this together. After overcoming all of these failures in our lives, constantly making our way back, grinding, fighting, and scrapping—she said, "There's no way we are going out like this. Not after what we've been through together." I'd like to tell you that at this moment I raised my fist in defiance and agreed, but that's not what I was thinking at all. All I was thinking was that I was going to die. Because it was true.

And even though I thought I was going to die, the number one rule of the Dan Bongino radio show is "don't get dead." And I did not want to get dead. And I couldn't break that rule.

I called my friend Sean Hannity (no, this isn't the name-dropping opportunity; he just really helped me out, and I want to shout him out) and said, "I need a favor." I think he thought I was going to ask about tickets to a football game or something. But that's not the way it turned out. "I've got this tumor on my neck," I told him. Anyone that tells you connections and friendships don't matter is full of shit. He knew everyone, and I knew he could help.

Sean got me in to see a couple of doctors. I had a biopsy done, and it was not good. One of the doctors said, "We're going have to cut you open, and we're going to have to take this out. Now. It's a serious surgery. We will cut your neck open and take the tumor out." And it wasn't small. It was a seven-centimeter tumor. "It's in a very delicate area, and I want to warn you," he continued, "lots of bad things potentially can happen. Vocal cords. Everything is at risk."

Everything is in your neck. It's the choke point—a funnel that everything flows through from brain to body.

Within days I was headed into surgery. And I was terrified about it.

What if he nicked a vocal cord? Again, no backup plan. This chapter opened up with me whining about aches and pains and now here we are. Something weird happened in the hospital as they prepped me to be cut open. One of the staff helping to administer an IV asked me what I did for a living. Usually, when people ask me what I do, I don't answer. I just figure, if you don't know me from what I do, it's not even worth explaining. One of my favorite pseudo-careers is being an "aqua dozer." What is an aqua dozer? I don't know. Someone told me they dug tunnels underwater once. However, once you say it, nobody asks any more questions. But this time I told the truth. She obviously didn't know who I was, so I simply said, "I do a podcast."

"It's not a political podcast, is it? You're not a Republican, are you?"

Holy shit, was this happening? Talk about a failure. I'm going to have this incredibly serious surgery, she's putting an IV in my hand (which hurts like crazy; I'm a big wuss with big needles), and she's asking me if I'm a Republican? She wasn't done either. She decided she was going to launch into an anti-Trump tirade, too, at the most inopportune time.

"Trump should've put a mask on...he helped COVID spread..." And on and on. Ordinarily, I would have started a fight over this, but I have to tell you, I was completely starved of energy. I thought, I could be dead in a few minutes, and this is not what I want to deal with on the way out.

It's interesting the way God intervenes in moments like this. I was down, and I couldn't believe this was happening. I was thinking, this is how far gone we are. This woman feels the need to make a political comment at this moment in my life. Folks, there's a word for this. It's called "discretion."

And then, just a few minutes later, my cell phone rang. "Dan, this is Donald Trump—your favorite president." Someone told him I was having surgery. And he called me. "Dan, I heard you are going to surgery. What can I do for you?" Folks, that's loyalty. And it's a two-way street. It was about the third or fourth time he had called me to let me know he was thinking about me. Trump understands the power of interpersonal dynamics better than anyone. Power asymmetries mean nothing to him. He was the president; I was a patient in the hospital. But he understood, and still understands the power of that personal touch. But this was also different. The timing felt like Divine Intervention. Literally. (And you know I *hate* that word). He rescued the moment. Thanks to President Trump, I was sent down to the surgery in a different emotional state. It was the one I needed to be in to help me survive all of this if things broke bad. I like to think I'm a thick-skinned, hard-nosed guy. But I can be a softy sometimes. And this was humbling.

Well, the surgeon was amazing, and not long after, I was back recording podcasts in the hotel room. The gravity of the moment did not hit me until soon after when Paula and I were flying back home to Florida.

It had been a whirlwind month. That's all the time that had passed since I found the lump and had been operated on. I was sitting in an aisle seat on the plane. Paula was in the center. Nothing had truly hit. There had been no time for self-pity or reflection, just fear and anxiety. But on that plane, it came at me like an avalanche. I was so exhausted. I had started researching Hodgkin's lymphoma the day I received a diagnosis from the doctor and discovered there was a five-year survival rate of about 80 percent. That crushed me. You might be thinking, why? Those odds are good. But are they? Remember, I had never anticipated any health problems, no less something with an 80 percent chance of survival. Still, after five years, twenty out of one hundred people die. I wasn't thinking about the 80 percent. I was thinking about the twenty who died. But it's all relative. There are a lot worse cancers than mine. When I went through treatment, I saw late-stage-five pancreatic cancer patients and others who I ran into at the various hospitals I was in all the time. After seeing thirteen-year-olds and sixty-year-olds with no hair, all just skin and bones, and all still fighting, you quickly throw away all the self-pity garbage. And all of a sudden, you start thinking again about that 80 percent who lived. It's all relative. Here I was, a guy in his midforties, with no health problems outside of some orthopedic issues, and now there's a 20 percent chance I wouldn't be here in five years?

It all hit me at once on that plane.

I'm not going to see my daughters get married. I'm not going to see my youngest daughter graduate high school.... Some truly weird thoughts started happening. Crazy shit goes through your head in a crisis like this: *They're building that new movie theater nearby my house, and I'll never see a movie there with Paula....* One minute you're thinking about your daughter's wedding, the next you're sweating over a cool new movie theater near your house.... I just started crying like a little kid. I lost it on the plane. I mean really bawling. Waterworks. This was not a single Kleenex episode. This was going to be close to an entire box. A guy was sitting across the aisle from me. I think he knew me from TV. He looked over to the left and gave me the "head nod" as if to say, "It will be okay, man." He saw me crying, and I thought, maybe it's going to be okay. *This guy seems to think so, so that's good. He looked smart, whatever that means.*

Sir, if you are reading this right now, thank you.

My official results came back as Hodgkin's lymphoma. It could have been worse. It could've been a far worse kind of cancer. I did chemo, which wasn't a lot of fun. If there was a consumer review site for chemo, I would definitely give it two thumbs down. Terrible reviews for chemo.

As of the writing of this book, I'm in remission. Thanks to the power of the Lord. But it could come back anytime, and if it does, I don't pretend to understand why the Lord makes these kinds of decisions. I'll always be at an elevated risk for cancer and the chemo does a number on your heart, so I'm now also at a higher risk for heart attack. But it is what it is. As I said earlier, none of this is supposed to be fair. That stuff is for kids' books.

People tell you these experiences change your outlook. I hope this never happens to you. But it does change you. It has to. If it doesn't, you're not paying attention. You start to realize some things are more valuable than the numbers in a bank account, downloads on a podcast, viewer eyeballs on a TV show, or votes in an election. There's breathing oxygen, and there's staying alive. There are your kids' soccer games and dropping your kid off at college (the latter of which was simultaneously the proudest and saddest day of my life—a dichotomy only a parent can understand).

Even though you might take good care of yourself—and I still do—nature or nurture or some combination of the two will eventually take over and throw you a curve ball. The bottom line is, my advice, don't wait for the diagnosis to live the life you want to live.

To do that would be the ultimate failure.

17

*"Don't think you are going to conceal faults
by concealing evidence that they ever existed."*

—DWIGHT D. EISENHOWER

I was connected to Rumble through Devin Nunes. He was and still is a good friend of mine, a former congressman of course. And he and I shared a mutual interest, not just in free speech, but in freeing the government from the shackles of the anti-Trump hysteria that was running so rampant.

He and I first came together over the Spygate story. Devin was one of the lead voices calling out the government's efforts to spy on Donald Trump early, and in a total failure of our media institutions, everybody laughed him off and called him a conspiracy theorist. So, to get around the inevitable censoring that was going to happen to his content due to his interest in getting the truth out, Devin decided to post his videos on Rumble. He made the introduction for me, figuring my early success with Parler could help the Rumble team out in building that platform as well.

I was eager to get off of YouTube because I wasn't going to get played again. At this point, I realized we were in a legitimate war, and I damn well better have a backup plan. If you were putting all of your stock in YouTube, Twitter, and Facebook at that point, you were just begging for it.

The writing was on the wall. Hell, it was also written in the sky, on highway signs, tattoos; it was every place. These were straight-up communists, and they didn't care how good you may have been for their business. If they hated your beliefs, you were gone.

So, I wasn't going to get burned again.

I connected with Rumble CEO Chris Pavlovski, and we hit it off. We kicked around some ideas about how to expand Rumble. He is an amazing guy. I admired many qualities of his. He wasn't a political guy; he just genuinely believed in this idea of creating a platform where everyone could speak freely. That sounds like a stupid sound bite that you throw into a book about a twelve-step program. But you have to understand that in the high-tech ecosystems that the libs run, this was rare. Tech people, by their liberal nature, were largely not interested in free speech. He was, which was amazing. So we negotiated and decided it would be a good idea if I took an equity stake in the company, because I cared about this. I wanted to help grow this flourishing parallel economy. As I have said before here, the best way to get skin in the game is to put skin in the game. It's one thing to just talk. It's another thing to risk your reputation on something.

Since I was now fully invested in Rumble, I kept using YouTube for one reason: to promote Rumble, figuring that this was going to come to a head soon. I knew my time was limited, and I wasn't going to censor myself on YouTube. So I took this period of about a year to promote Rumble on YouTube, to send the biggest "fuck you" to the platform that I could. I would talk about whatever I wanted, and whenever YouTube put out a COVID admonition saying, "You can't talk about this," I would talk about it twice, just to piss them off.

I knew that this was going to come to a head. But it was a glorious year. There was nothing better than beating YouTube at its own censorship game. Going on a censorship platform, while promoting an alternative to censorship, was a slice of heaven.

I know this is a chapter on Rumble but as I told you in the lead-up to this, this was built out of rage and a reckoning at this point, so allow me to rage against YouTube for just a little bit more.

I knew this would come to an end soon: me shitting all over them and daring them to ban me. And they did. Paula and I were on a flight up to New York when I got an email from a lady named Coco, some kind of YouTube PR representative.

It was a pleasantly worded email that basically said, "We're suspending your account along with the monetization power of your account. We're taking action against your account." It was because of my stances on COVID and of course, she said I had no recourse. They never give you that, despite what they may say.

This is how Business Insider reported the news in part:

> The popular conservative pundit Dan Bongino has been temporarily suspended from YouTube for spreading misinformation about COVID-19. A YouTube spokesperson told The Hill on Friday that Bongino was banned from posting videos for a week after he claimed in a video that masks are "useless" in stopping the spread of the virus.

So I was thinking, okay, this is that moment I've been waiting for. They were about to ban me for suggesting what is now scientifically accurate information about masks and vaccines.

So instead of sitting back and just riding off into the sunset, I thought it would be a good opportunity to screenshot Coco's email and send it all over the digital universe to show everyone else how these thugs operate. Then, we decided to do a dedication song to her on my radio show, courtesy of my producer, Jim: "Coco's Greatest Hits." It was hilarious. I still listen to it when I need a laugh.

Of course, Coco probably didn't like that. My experience with these people is that they can dish it out, but they can't take it. So we decided it was time to finally part ways with YouTube. The account wasn't completely suspended, but the last video I recorded was titled "Why I'm leaving YouTube" because I wanted to be sure that the public knew what was going on. I knew that YouTube would pull out the typical "You can't quit, you're fired" kind of thing, so I recorded the video so that everybody would know the real score.

I put it on YouTube and explained why I was leaving, stating that YouTube is a mercenary communist company. Of course, they banned my account and wiped the video account history clean. So now I had this trillion-dollar company by the balls—which led a bunch of liberals to write about the ban—which inadvertently led to people joining Rumble. Millions of dollars of free advertising for YouTube's competitor. Glorious. And yet, so stupid. Here you had a $1 trillion company with zero understanding of PR. It all just blew up in their faces. I got tons of emails from people creating Rumble accounts; it was lots of engagement from those who realized I had been targeted.

Subscribers on my Rumble account also went through the roof.

The "negation" was working on YouTube just as it had with Parler. "We were not YouTube." John Stockton, the greatest assist king in NBA history, had nothing on these people when it came to the big assist. By behaving as they were, YouTube was driving our business. They should've just let conservatives do their thing and enforce some simple, basic moderation rules. Instead, they facilitated Rumble and other alternate tech platforms in the future, because like small children, they couldn't control themselves. They let emotions get in the way of common sense.

It's like Fox News. It took them ten years to get to number one and stay there, and I think we will look back in ten years at tech companies and look at what CNN, MSNBC, and the major networks with the far left did with their radical coverage. We will look back at Parler and Rumble and see that it was nuclear fission, where the "media atom" broke apart. The technology book of Genesis.

We may never be YouTube. It may take ten years, and we may not have as many bells and whistles as they do, but the hard reality is, most people just want to watch content. They just want to be left alone to be entertained and/or informed. Did they get rid of me because of my stance on masks? They said they did, but no. They got rid of me because I'm Dan Bongino. All big tech had to do was just ignore the Ben & Jerry's eaters, but they couldn't do that. That was their failure and that failure helped us. What we learned from their failure was how to grow.

I still use Twitter. I still use Facebook. When Elon Musk purchased Twitter, the left played the victim. It's hilarious. They still can't get enough of sticking it to you. Or at least trying to. They derive some kind of pleasure from attacking and hurting and insulting conservatives. It's weird, but it's real.

I can tell you with the straightest of faces and the purest of hearts I don't want to hurt anybody. I don't want anybody to be fired for their political views. I worked in the Secret Service with Democrats and Republicans. Do you know what we did together? We protected the president, and we left our politics at the door. The fact that the left wants to see you in pain so badly is perverse. They're grotesque. They have this bloodthirsty desire to destroy people. They have a childlike lack of self-control that will most likely be the death of their own brands. We're seeing it every day. Acts of self-destruction everywhere. But hey, it's a free country. Let them self-destruct. No problem. We are living in the free-speech industrial revolution and anything now goes.

One last point in all of this: It's never been a good idea to create two companies that do the exact same thing. It's redundant. But that's not the world we live in. In the world we live in, we have to create duplicates of everything to escape the totalitarians on the left. It's a lot of wasted efficiencies, a lot of recreating the obvious. But think of how wasteful wars are, both real and ideological. The choice is to go with efficiencies and be censored or go create your own and play by your own rules.

Yes, it's redundant. But at least you will live in freedom. Look, every American is punished by big tech failures when they look to shut down opposing voices.

The Pink Floyd album *The Wall* loops on itself from the last seconds of the last song and continues into the first seconds of the first song. That's where we are right now as this book approaches its close. This is where we came in. Ringing the bell as Rumble became a billion-dollar company. Even after all of these repeated bouts of failure, we still rang that bell. The fight for free speech gave birth to Rumble's biggest successes. But had I not failed with YouTube, it may not have played out the same way. When certain entities look to shut down the voice of the people, whether that be you, me, or our worst enemies, that's the most important time to stand up. That's the most important time to take these failures and use them as weapons against the opposition. If I've learned anything, it's the importance that anything worth offending is a thing that's worth defending. With your own skin in the game. With your own heart in the fight.

Afterword

I'd like to leave you with something I wrote at the end of 2022 and posted on social media. It became one of the most, if not *the* most, shared pieces of personal writing that I have ever posted. It has to do with failure, but it also has to do with life in general, and I hope you appreciate the spirit with which it is intended.

I also want to thank each of you for holding this book right now, even you libs who decided to give these stories a chance. In fact, I'd like to give the libs a little extra shout-out because I'm sure it took a lot of guts to read something by me. I respect that. Look, at the end of the day, we are all just people trying to figure things out. Hopefully, as we fight for what we believe in, we do so fairly, honestly, and with the integrity that comes with true conviction. Don't get me wrong. You try and shut me or anybody else down when it comes to free expression, I will do whatever I can to counter your arguments and make you pay. But as far as defending people who I don't agree with? I'm there. I'll fight for your rights just like I will the rights of any conservatives or anything in between. But I won't defend your right to take that right away from others. That's not what this country was built upon. The defining element that makes the United States, in my opinion, the single most important nation in the history of the world is the concept of freedom of expression. To not defend that would be the ultimate failure.

And it will never happen on my watch.

I hope you all feel at least a little bit more motivated to go out into the world, speak your truth, respect others as they do the same, and most importantly, use your failures to push yourself to the next level. As I have learned time and again, failures are the lifeblood of any decent and thoughtful advocate, spouse, parent, friend, entrepreneur...anyone and everyone.

With that, here's the post I referenced a few paragraphs ago:

As we approach another new year, here's some life advice I wish I could give my younger self:

1) Grit and determination are far more determinative of success than intelligence, looks, or athleticism. I've met a lot of very smart people who stumbled and simply failed to get up. The world is littered with gifted people who failed to get up after the fall. They don't see failure as a gift to learn from, but an insurmountable obstacle. Look around, you'll see these people everywhere and you'll never unsee it. And then look at the gritty people—chances are they've had incredible failures before their most profound achievements.

2) A formal education is largely worthless with regard to skill training, outside of a few extremely specialized fields. There's very little a person can't learn with intense, on-the-job training. However, a formal education can be extremely useful for developing critical soft skills such as time management, public speaking, and writing. It's also beneficial to learn the jargon of academia. Smart people like to remind others (and themselves) that they're smart. They use jargon as a password to "the club." The more passwords you know, the better.

3) If you're not taking some measure to take care of your health then you're not optimizing your brief existence on this rock. Frequent, intense, but manageable exercise should be priority number one for your success. A healthy body and brain will change your outlook on everything. It'll also allow you to fight the inevitable damage of time while others wither away faster. This also applies to your diet. You don't have to live a Spartan lifestyle with regard to what you eat, but the established, well-researched benefits of the nutrients in vegetables, fruits, and healthy meats are undeniable. Ignore them at your own peril because what you eat will NOT ignore you.

4) Sleep is the game changer. Show me someone sleeping four hours a night and I'll show you half the person they should've been. Deep sleep is critical to healing the body and the brain. It's a complete game changer when you figure this out.

5) View your life as if you're watching a movie of it. Are you proud of the character in the movie? Or ashamed? I make a lot of mistakes but when I'm about to make another one I use this simple trick.

6) Spend as much time with your kids as you can. NO ONE dies wishing they'd spent less time with their children. No one.

7) Choose your friends wisely. You don't need a lot of friends. But you do need a few very good ones. Being able to trust another human being who you are not related to, with your troubles and secrets, helps keep you from imploding from the pressure of holding it all in.

8) Finally. Never, ever, waste substantial amounts of time. Every second is an opportunity to improve your mind, your body, or a relationship with someone else. Time obviously doesn't stop for anyone and every second lost is in the abyss.

THE GIFT OF FAILURE

*Even watching television on a day off provides an opportu-
nity to learn something new, to learn a new "password." Relax
when you hit the redline, but other than that don't waste time.*

Gifts of Failure

A gift of failure: The power of self-reflection. When we experience failure, it can be easy to get caught up in negative emotions and self-doubt. However, taking the time to reflect on what went wrong and why can help us gain valuable insights into our own behaviors and thought patterns. I'm not naïve. Neither are you. This is really easy to talk and write about in a book, but in the middle of a traumatic situation, in that black cloud, it can be hard to shake. But just because it's difficult doesn't mean it's not worth a commitment to try, and like any skill, you'll get better at focusing on the problems that are solvable rather than the emotions that aren't as you pick yourself up off the mat after each failure.

A gift of failure: Persistence. Every few years, there's a new euphemism for persistence; maybe grit, drive, determination, which are all perfectly viable and appropriate words. Whenever someone needs to sell a new book, they basically replace the word persistence with something else to sell more copies. That's fine. I don't care what word you use—right now I'm calling it persistence. A lot of these books share one common theme. Persistence. Failure can be discouraging and disheartening, but giving up after the first setback or obstacle will only prevent us from achieving our goals. That's why persistence matters. A lot of successful people are the way they are because they didn't give up in the face of failure. I'm sure there'll be a new euphemism in a few years by someone else to sell another couple thousand copies of their book. But the hard reality is: it makes sense. Persistence is a critical trait for success in any area of life, and failure can teach us the importance of sticking with it even when things get tough.

A gift of failure: Learning the value of taking calculated risks. I don't want you to get the impression from this book when I say things like "Bet on yourself" and "Get up off the mat" that you should do stupid things and they'll all be solved by dusting off your elbows, head, and knees and getting back up to fight the fight. Sometimes when a Mike Tyson type hits you in the face and you're on the mat, it's just best to stay down and take the ten-count. I'm not saying don't take risks. But take *good* risks. Do your homework. Do the math. If you're going to take risks, at least be sure you put in the time first to minimize any potential damage if it doesn't work out. Better to know far in advance what you can calculate into your risk equation on what you're going to do or decide not to do, rather than to be surprised later.

A gift of failure: Learning how to be more resilient. Failure can be incredibly discouraging and demotivating, but if we learn to bounce back from setbacks and keep trying, we can develop resilience. This can be a valuable skill in all aspects of life, as it helps us to overcome challenges and obstacles and to stay focused on our goals. By learning from our mistakes, reflecting on what went wrong, and adapting our approach, we can become more resilient and better equipped to handle whatever life throws our way.

A gift of failure: Learning how to "reframe." Have you ever noticed how a picture, the same picture, looks really different when you just change the framing or the matting? The picture hasn't changed at all, just what surrounds it. Well, failures are the same way. My journey in this book has been a learning experience for me. Some of the things I initially had in the outline as failures, interestingly enough, when I wrote them, I saw in a different light. Obviously, retrospectively, you get to see things differently due to the benefits of the chronological passage of time. But you can reframe something not as a failure but as an opportunity to not make the same mistake again and as kind of a launching pad to something different and possibly better. One of the most deeply impactful books in my life was Viktor Frankl's *Man's Search for Meaning*, where he comes to the conclusion, after describing life in Nazi death camps, that the meaning we all have in life is hope. And for me, hope, that belief that things can still get better, is a great new "frame" to hang around a failure.

The gift of failure: Learning that failure is not the end of the road. Failure is not a reflection of our worth or abilities but rather an opportunity to learn, grow, and improve. When we fail, we are forced to confront our mistakes and weaknesses, which can be uncomfortable and humbling. Candidly, this is still a failure I'm dealing with now. Humility can be a gift too. It pains me to say this, but I struggle with this now. You never want to open up to people in a book, even if it's your own, and tell people that you have these moments where you're acting like an egomaniac. It's embarrassing and it's stupid and nobody likes that. But yes, I've had these problems too. I'll fail again. And the gift of failure in this case is that it levels you out and makes sure you don't get high on your own stash, and then helps you become better equipped to handle the learning phase as you confront your mistakes and weaknesses.

A gift of failure: Learning that we should not let it define our self-worth. This is probably one of the most valuable lessons of the book, if not *the* most valuable. It's equally important to remember that our worth as individuals is not solely determined like a spreadsheet of successes versus failures. It's easy to get caught up in the idea that failures define us, but this mindset can be damaging to our mental health and overall well-being. The hard reality is just like baseball. Even the best hitters sometimes fail seven out of ten times. And no one's going to tell you a .300 hitter in baseball has no worth. If you allow the failure solely to define you, you'll be encompassed by this black cloud of negativity and you'll lose hope.

The gift of failure: Learning the importance of having a growth mindset. A growth mindset means believing that our abilities and skills can be developed through hard work and dedication, rather than being fixed traits that cannot be changed. When we fail, it can be easy to fall into a fixed mindset and believe that our abilities are limited. However, by adopting a growth mindset, we can view failure as an opportunity to learn and grow rather than a reflection of our innate abilities. By doing so, we can cultivate a sense of curiosity, a willingness to learn, and a resilience to setbacks. Ultimately, having a growth mindset can help us to achieve greater success and fulfillment in all areas of our lives.

A gift of failure: Learning how to embrace change. Failure often occurs when our plans and strategies do not work out as intended, and we must be willing to adapt to new circumstances in order to overcome our challenges. Embracing change means having the flexibility to adjust our approach, try new things, and make changes as needed. I recently read a story about how the next generation of employees, the twenty-somethings, now actually crave stability over income when choosing their next careers. I was horrified by this story. The only thing stable about a job, the job market, and the economy is its instability. And my fear here is we're developing a bunch of rigid automatons, unable to embrace this principle of embracing change.

A gift of failure: Learning how to seek feedback and learn from others. When we fail, it can be helpful to seek out feedback from others who can offer a different perspective and help us to identify areas for improvement. By doing so, we can learn from our mistakes and make the necessary changes to improve our performance in the future. Seeking feedback also helps us to build relationships and foster a culture of continuous learning and growth. Ultimately, those who are open to feedback and willing to learn from others are often the ones who go on to achieve the greatest success.